2017 SQA Past Papers & Hodder Gibson Model Paper with Answers

Advanced Higher
MATHEMATICS

2015 Specimen Question Paper,
Model Paper, 2016 & 2017 Exams

HODDER
GIBSON
AN HACHETTE UK COMPANY

This book contains the official 2015 SQA Specimen Question Paper and the 2016 and 2017 Exams for Advanced Higher Maths, with associated SQA-approved answers modified from the official marking instructions that accompany the paper.

In addition the book contains a model paper, together with answers, plus study skills advice. This paper, which may include a limited number of previously published SQA questions, has been specially commissioned by Hodder Gibson, and has been written by experienced senior teachers and examiners in line with the Advanced Higher for CfE syllabus and assessment outlines. This is not SQA material but has been devised to provide further practice for Advanced Higher examinations.

Hodder Gibson is grateful to the copyright holders, as credited on the final page of the Answer section, for permission to use their material. Every effort has been made to trace the copyright holders and to obtain their permission for the use of copyright material. Hodder Gibson will be happy to receive information allowing us to rectify any error or omission in future editions.

Hachette UK's policy is to use papers that are natural, renewable and recyclable products and made from wood grown in sustainable forests. The logging and manufacturing processes are expected to conform to the environmental regulations of the country of origin.

Orders: please contact Bookpoint Ltd, 130 Park Drive, Milton Park, Abingdon, Oxon OX14 4SE. Telephone: (44) 01235 827720. Fax: (44) 01235 400454. Lines are open 9.00–5.00, Monday to Saturday, with a 24-hour message answering service. Visit our website at www.hoddereducation.co.uk. Hodder Gibson can be contacted direct on: Tel: 0141 333 4650; Fax: 0141 404 8188; email: hoddergibson@hodder.co.uk

This collection first published in 2017 by
Hodder Gibson, an imprint of Hodder Education,
An Hachette UK Company
211 St Vincent Street
Glasgow G2 5QY

Typeset by Aptara, Inc.

Printed in the UK

A catalogue record for this title is available from the British Library

ISBN: 978-1-5104-2135-6

2 1

2018 2017

Introduction

Study Skills – what you need to know to pass exams!

Pause for thought

Many students might skip quickly through a page like this. After all, we all know how to revise. Do you really though?

Think about this:

"IF YOU ALWAYS DO WHAT YOU ALWAYS DO, YOU WILL ALWAYS GET WHAT YOU HAVE ALWAYS GOT."

Do you like the grades you get? Do you want to do better? If you get full marks in your assessment, then that's great! Change nothing! This section is just to help you get that little bit better than you already are.

There are two main parts to the advice on offer here. The first part highlights fairly obvious things but which are also very important. The second part makes suggestions about revision that you might not have thought about but which WILL help you.

Part 1

DOH! It's so obvious but …

Start revising in good time

Don't leave it until the last minute – this will make you panic.

Make a revision timetable that sets out work time AND play time.

Sleep and eat!

Obvious really, and very helpful. Avoid arguments or stressful things too – even games that wind you up. You need to be fit, awake and focused!

Know your place!

Make sure you know exactly **WHEN and WHERE** your exams are.

Know your enemy!

Make sure you know what to expect in the exam.

How is the paper structured?

How much time is there for each question?

What types of question are involved?

Which topics seem to come up time and time again?

Which topics are your strongest and which are your weakest?

Are all topics compulsory or are there choices?

Learn by DOING!

There is no substitute for past papers and practice papers – they are simply essential! Tackling this collection of papers and answers is exactly the right thing to be doing as your exams approach.

Part 2

People learn in different ways. Some like low light, some bright. Some like early morning, some like evening / night. Some prefer warm, some prefer cold. But everyone uses their BRAIN and the brain works when it is active. Passive learning – sitting gazing at notes – is the most INEFFICIENT way to learn anything. Below you will find tips and ideas for making your revision more effective and maybe even more enjoyable. What follows gets your brain active, and active learning works!

Activity 1 – Stop and review

Step 1

When you have done no more than 5 minutes of revision reading STOP!

Step 2

Write a heading in your own words which sums up the topic you have been revising.

Step 3

Write a summary of what you have revised in no more than two sentences. Don't fool yourself by saying, "I know it, but I cannot put it into words". That just means you don't know it well enough. If you cannot write your summary, revise that section again, knowing that you must write a summary at the end of it. Many of you will have notebooks full of blue/black ink writing. Many of the pages will not be especially attractive or memorable so try to liven them up a bit with colour as you are reviewing and rewriting. **This is a great memory aid, and memory is the most important thing.**

Activity 2 – Use technology!

Why should everything be written down? Have you thought about "mental" maps, diagrams, cartoons and colour to help you learn? And rather than write down notes, why not record your revision material?

What about having a text message revision session with friends? Keep in touch with them to find out how and what they are revising and share ideas and questions.

Why not make a video diary where you tell the camera what you are doing, what you think you have learned and what you still have to do? No one has to see or hear it, but the process of having to organise your thoughts in a formal way to explain something is a very important learning practice.

Be sure to make use of electronic files. You could begin to summarise your class notes. Your typing might be slow, but it will get faster and the typed notes will be easier to read than the scribbles in your class notes. Try to add different fonts and colours to make your work stand out. You can easily Google relevant pictures, cartoons and diagrams which you can copy and paste to make your work more attractive and **MEMORABLE**.

Activity 3 – This is it. Do this and you will know lots!

Step 1

In this task you must be very honest with yourself! Find the SQA syllabus for your subject (www.sqa.org.uk). Look at how it is broken down into main topics called MANDATORY knowledge. That means stuff you MUST know.

Step 2

BEFORE you do ANY revision on this topic, write a list of everything that you already know about the subject. It might be quite a long list but you only need to write it once. It shows you all the information that is already in your long-term memory so you know what parts you do not need to revise!

Step 3

Pick a chapter or section from your book or revision notes. Choose a fairly large section or a whole chapter to get the most out of this activity.

With a buddy, use Skype, Facetime, Twitter or any other communication you have, to play the game "If this is the answer, what is the question?". For example, if you are revising Geography and the answer you provide is "meander", your buddy would have to make up a question like "What is the word that describes a feature of a river where it flows slowly and bends often from side to side?".

Make up 10 "answers" based on the content of the chapter or section you are using. Give this to your buddy to solve while you solve theirs.

Step 4

Construct a wordsearch of at least 10 × 10 squares. You can make it as big as you like but keep it realistic. Work together with a group of friends. Many apps allow you to make wordsearch puzzles online. The words and phrases can go in any direction and phrases can be split. Your puzzle must only contain facts linked to the topic you are revising. Your task is to find 10 bits of information to hide in your puzzle, but you must not repeat information that you used in Step 3. DO NOT show where the words are. Fill up empty squares with random letters. Remember to keep a note of where your answers are hidden but do not show your friends. When you have a complete puzzle, exchange it with a friend to solve each other's puzzle.

Step 5

Now make up 10 questions (not "answers" this time) based on the same chapter used in the previous two tasks. Again, you must find NEW information that you have not yet used. Now it's getting hard to find that new information! Again, give your questions to a friend to answer.

Step 6

As you have been doing the puzzles, your brain has been actively searching for new information. Now write a NEW LIST that contains only the new information you have discovered when doing the puzzles. Your new list is the one to look at repeatedly for short bursts over the next few days. Try to remember more and more of it without looking at it. After a few days, you should be able to add words from your second list to your first list as you increase the information in your long-term memory.

FINALLY! Be inspired...

Make a list of different revision ideas and beside each one write **THINGS I HAVE** tried, **THINGS I WILL** try and **THINGS I MIGHT** try. Don't be scared of trying something new.

And remember – "FAIL TO PREPARE AND PREPARE TO FAIL!"

Advanced Higher Mathematics

The course

The Advanced Higher Mathematics course is designed to build upon and extend the skills, knowledge and understanding that you have attained in the Higher Mathematics course (or equivalent qualification). It enables you to develop further skills in calculus, algebra and geometry. Areas such as number theory, complex numbers and matrices are introduced as well as processes of rigorous proof.

How the course is assessed

To gain the course award, you must pass the three Units:

- Methods in Algebra and Calculus
- Applications of Algebra and Calculus
- Geometry, Proof and Systems of Equations

as well as the examination.

The Units are assessed internally on a pass/fail basis.

The examination is set and marked by experienced practitioners appointed by SQA.

The course award is graded A–D, the grade being determined by the total mark you score in the examination.

The examination

The examination is a three-hour paper with a total of 100 marks, in which the use of a calculator is permitted. A formulae list will be provided (see page two of the specimen question paper).

The question paper consists of short- and extended-response questions that require the application of skills developed in the course. You are expected to communicate responses clearly and to justify solutions.

Further details can be found in the Advanced Higher Mathematics section on the SQA website: www.sqa.org.uk/sqa/48507.html.

Key tips for your success

Practise! Practise! Practise!

DOING maths questions is the most effective use of your study time. You will benefit much more from spending 30 minutes doing maths questions than spending several hours copying out notes or reading a maths textbook. Practise basic skills such as the product and quotient rules regularly.

Prior learning

Ensure that you know trigonometric identities and other relevant formulae from the Higher Mathematics course, as well as essential basic techniques such as solving quadratic equations.

Show all working clearly

The instructions on the front of the exam paper state that "Full credit will be given only to solutions which contain appropriate working." A "correct" answer with no working may only be awarded partial marks or even no marks at all. An incomplete answer will be awarded marks for any appropriate working.

Attempt every question, even if you are not sure whether you are correct or not. Your solution may contain working which will gain some marks. A blank response is certain to be awarded no marks.

Never cross out working unless you have something better to replace it with.

Ensure that you communicate reasons for what you have done, wherever appropriate. In particular, in proof and "show that" questions, include all lines of working.

Marking instructions

Ensure that you look at the detailed marking instructions of model papers and past papers. They provide further advice and guidelines as well as showing you precisely where, and for what, marks are awarded.

Extended response questions

You should look for connections between parts of questions, particularly where there are three or four sections to a question. These are almost always linked and, in some instances, an earlier result in part (a) or (b) is needed and its use would avoid further repeated work.

Accuracy

Where possible use exact values; decimal approximations may lead to inaccuracies which could cost you marks.

Notation

In all questions make sure that you use the correct notation. In particular, for integration questions, remember to include '*dx*' within your integral. When finding an indefinite integral, remember to include the constant of integration in your answer.

Radians

Remember to work in radians when attempting any question involving both trigonometry and calculus.

Simplify

Get into the habit of simplifying expressions before doing any further work with them. This should make all subsequent work easier.

Good luck!

Remember that the rewards for passing Advanced Higher Mathematics are well worth it! Your pass will help you get the future you want for yourself. In the exam, be confident in your own ability; if you're not sure how to answer a question, trust your instincts and give it a go anyway – keep calm and don't panic! GOOD LUCK!

National
Qualifications
SPECIMEN ONLY

Mathematics

Duration — 3 hours

Total marks — 100

Attempt ALL questions.

You may use a calculator.

Full credit will be given only to solutions which contain appropriate working.

State the units for your answer where appropriate.

Write your answers clearly in the answer booklet provided. In the answer booklet, you must clearly identify the question number you are attempting.

Use **blue** or **black** ink.

Before leaving the examination room you must give your answer booklet to the Invigilator; if you do not, you may lose all the marks for this paper.

FORMULAE LIST

Standard derivatives		Standard integrals	
$f(x)$	$f'(x)$	$f(x)$	$\int f(x)\,dx$
$\sin^{-1}x$	$\dfrac{1}{\sqrt{1-x^2}}$	$\sec^2(ax)$	$\dfrac{1}{a}\tan(ax)+c$
$\cos^{-1}x$	$-\dfrac{1}{\sqrt{1-x^2}}$	$\dfrac{1}{\sqrt{a^2-x^2}}$	$\sin^{-1}\left(\dfrac{x}{a}\right)+c$
$\tan^{-1}x$	$\dfrac{1}{1+x^2}$	$\dfrac{1}{a^2+x^2}$	$\dfrac{1}{a}\tan^{-1}\left(\dfrac{x}{a}\right)+c$
$\tan x$	$\sec^2 x$	$\dfrac{1}{x}$	$\ln|x|+c$
$\cot x$	$-\operatorname{cosec}^2 x$	e^{ax}	$\dfrac{1}{a}e^{ax}+c$
$\sec x$	$\sec x\tan x$		
$\operatorname{cosec} x$	$-\operatorname{cosec} x\cot x$		
$\ln x$	$\dfrac{1}{x}$		
e^x	e^x		

Summations

(Arithmetic series) $S_n = \dfrac{1}{2}n[2a+(n-1)d]$

(Geometric series) $S_n = \dfrac{a(1-r^n)}{1-r}$

$$\sum_{r=1}^{n} r = \frac{n(n+1)}{2}, \quad \sum_{r=1}^{n} r^2 = \frac{n(n+1)(2n+1)}{6}, \quad \sum_{r=1}^{n} r^3 = \frac{n^2(n+1)^2}{4}$$

Binomial theorem

$$(a+b)^n = \sum_{r=0}^{n} \binom{n}{r} a^{n-r}b^r \quad \text{where} \quad \binom{n}{r} = {}^nC_r = \frac{n!}{r!(n-r)!}$$

Maclaurin expansion

$$f(x) = f(0) + f'(0)x + \frac{f''(0)x^2}{2!} + \frac{f'''(0)x^3}{3!} + \frac{f^{iv}(0)x^4}{4!} + \dots$$

De Moivre's theorem

$$[r(\cos\theta + i\sin\theta)]^n = r^n(\cos n\theta + i\sin n\theta)$$

Vector product

$$\mathbf{a} \times \mathbf{b} = |\mathbf{a}||\mathbf{b}|\sin\theta\,\hat{\mathbf{n}} = \begin{vmatrix} \mathbf{i} & \mathbf{j} & \mathbf{k} \\ a_1 & a_2 & a_3 \\ b_1 & b_2 & b_3 \end{vmatrix} = \mathbf{i}\begin{vmatrix} a_2 & a_3 \\ b_2 & b_3 \end{vmatrix} - \mathbf{j}\begin{vmatrix} a_1 & a_3 \\ b_1 & b_3 \end{vmatrix} + \mathbf{k}\begin{vmatrix} a_1 & a_2 \\ b_1 & b_2 \end{vmatrix}$$

Matrix transformation

Anti-clockwise rotation through an angle, θ about the origin, $\begin{bmatrix} \cos\theta & -\sin\theta \\ \sin\theta & \cos\theta \end{bmatrix}$

Total marks — 100

MARKS

Attempt ALL questions

1. Given $f(x) = \dfrac{x-1}{1+x^2}$, show that $f'(x) = \dfrac{1+2x-x^2}{(1+x^2)^2}$.

   3

2. State and simplify the general term in the binomial expansion of $\left(2x - \dfrac{5}{x^2}\right)^6$.

   Hence, or otherwise, find the term independent of x.

   3

3. Find $\displaystyle\int \frac{2}{\sqrt{9-16x^2}}\, dx$.

   3

4. Show that the greatest common divisor of 487 and 729 is 1.

   Hence find integers x and y such that $487x + 729y = 1$.

   4

5. Find $\displaystyle\int x^2 e^{3x}\, dx$.

   5

6. Find the values of the constant k for which the matrix $\begin{pmatrix} 3 & k & 2 \\ 3 & -4 & 2 \\ k & 0 & 1 \end{pmatrix}$ is singular.

   4

7. A spherical balloon is being inflated. When the radius is 10 cm the surface area is increasing at a rate of $120\pi\,\mathrm{cm}^2\,\mathrm{s}^{-1}$.

   Find the rate at which the volume is increasing at this moment.

   5

   (Volume of sphere $= \dfrac{4}{3}\pi r^3$, surface area $= 4\pi r^2$)

8. (a) Find the Maclaurin expansions up to and including the term in x^3, simplifying the coefficients as far as possible, for the following:

   (i) $f(x) = e^{3x}$

   (ii) $g(x) = (x+2)^{-2}$

   5

   (b) Given that $h(x) = \dfrac{xe^{3x}}{(x+2)^2}$ use the expansions from (a) to approximate the value

   of $h\left(\dfrac{1}{2}\right)$.

   3

MARKS

9. Three terms of an arithmetic sequence, u_3, u_7 and u_{16} form the first three terms of a geometric sequence.

   Show that $a = \dfrac{6}{5}d$, where a and d are, respectively, the first term and common difference of the arithmetic sequence with $d \neq 0$.

   Hence, or otherwise, find the value of r, the common ratio of the geometric sequence.   **4**

10. Using logarithmic differentiation, or otherwise, find $\dfrac{dy}{dx}$ given that

$$e^y = \frac{(3x+2)e^{2x}}{(2x-1)^2}, \quad x > \frac{1}{2}.$$ **3**

11. Find the exact value of $\displaystyle\int_1^2 \frac{x+4}{(x+1)^2(2x-1)}\,dx$.   **7**

12. (a) Given that m and n are positive integers state the negation of the statement:

   m is even or n is even.   **1**

   (b) By considering the contrapositive of the following statement:

   if mn is even then m is even or n is even,

   prove that the statement is true for all positive integers m and n.   **3**

13. Consider the curve in the (x, y) plane defined by the equation $y = \dfrac{4x-3}{x^2-2x-8}$.

   (a) Identify the vertical asymptotes to this curve and justify your answer.   **2**

   Here are two statements about the curve:

   (1) It does not cross or touch the x-axis.

   (2) The line $y = 0$ is an asymptote.

   (b) (i) State why statement (1) is false.

   (ii) Show that statement (2) is true.   **3**

MARKS

14. The lines L_1 and L_2 are given by the following equations:

$$L_1: \frac{x+6}{3} = \frac{y-1}{-1} = \frac{z-2}{2}$$

$$L_2: \frac{x+5}{4} = \frac{y+4}{1} = \frac{z}{4}$$

(a) Show that the lines L_1 and L_2 intersect and state the coordinates of the point of intersection.   **5**

(b) Find the equation of the plane containing L_1 and L_2.   **3**

A third line, L_3, is given by the equation $\frac{x-1}{2} = \frac{y+7}{4} = \frac{z-3}{-1}$.

(c) Calculate the acute angle between L_3 and the plane. Give your answer in degrees correct to 2 decimal places.   **4**

15. (a) Given that $f(x) = \ln\left(\frac{1+x}{1-x}\right)$, find $f'(x)$, expressing your answer as a single fraction.   **2**

(b) Solve the differential equation

$$\cos x \frac{dy}{dx} + y \tan x = \frac{\cos x}{e^{\sec x}}$$

given that $y = 1$ when $x = 2\pi$. Express your answer in the form $y = f(x)$.   **7**

16. Let $S_n = \sum_{r=1}^{n} \frac{1}{r(r+1)}$ where n is a positive integer.

(a) Prove that, for all positive integers n, $S_n = \frac{n}{n+1}$.   **5**

(b) Find

(i) the least value of n such that $S_{n+1} - S_n < \frac{1}{1000}$

(ii) the value of n for which $S_n \times S_{n-1} \times S_{n-2} = S_{n-8}$.   **5**

MARKS

17. (a) Given $z = \cos\theta + i\sin\theta$, use de Moivre's theorem and the binomial theorem to show that:

$$\cos 4\theta = \cos^4\theta - 6\cos^2\theta\sin^2\theta + \sin^4\theta$$

and

$$\sin 4\theta = 4\cos^3\theta\sin\theta - 4\cos\theta\sin^3\theta.$$

5

(b) Hence show that $\tan 4\theta = \dfrac{4\tan\theta - 4\tan^3\theta}{1 - 6\tan^2\theta + \tan^4\theta}$.

3

(c) Find algebraically the solutions to the equation

$$\tan^4\theta + 4\tan^3\theta - 6\tan^2\theta - 4\tan\theta + 1 = 0$$

in the interval $0 \leq \theta \leq \dfrac{\pi}{2}$.

3

[END OF SPECIMEN QUESTION PAPER]

[BLANK PAGE]

ADVANCED HIGHER

Model Paper

Whilst this Model Paper has been specially commissioned by Hodder Gibson for use as practice for the Advanced Higher (for Curriculum for Excellence) exams, the key reference document remains the SQA Specimen Paper 2015 and the SQA Past Papers 2016 and 2017.

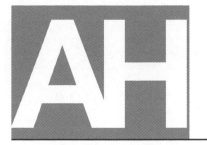

National
Qualifications
MODEL PAPER

Mathematics

Duration — 3 hours

Total marks — 100

Attempt ALL questions.

You may use a calculator.

Full credit will be given only to solutions which contain appropriate working.

State the units for your answer where appropriate.

Write your answers clearly in the answer booklet provided. In the answer booklet, you must clearly identify the question number you are attempting.

Use **blue** or **black** ink.

Before leaving the examination room you must give your answer booklet to the Invigilator; if you do not, you may lose all the marks for this paper.

FORMULAE LIST

Standard derivatives		Standard integrals	
$f(x)$	$f'(x)$	$f(x)$	$\int f(x)\,dx$
$\sin^{-1}x$	$\dfrac{1}{\sqrt{1-x^2}}$	$\sec^2(ax)$	$\dfrac{1}{a}\tan(ax)+c$
$\cos^{-1}x$	$-\dfrac{1}{\sqrt{1-x^2}}$	$\dfrac{1}{\sqrt{a^2-x^2}}$	$\sin^{-1}\left(\dfrac{x}{a}\right)+c$
$\tan^{-1}x$	$\dfrac{1}{1+x^2}$	$\dfrac{1}{a^2+x^2}$	$\dfrac{1}{a}\tan^{-1}\left(\dfrac{x}{a}\right)+c$
$\tan x$	$\sec^2 x$	$\dfrac{1}{x}$	$\ln|x|+c$
$\cot x$	$-\operatorname{cosec}^2 x$	e^{ax}	$\dfrac{1}{a}e^{ax}+c$
$\sec x$	$\sec x \tan x$		
$\operatorname{cosec} x$	$-\operatorname{cosec} x \cot x$		
$\ln x$	$\dfrac{1}{x}$		
e^x	e^x		

Summations

(Arithmetic series) $\qquad S_n = \dfrac{1}{2}n[2a+(n-1)d]$

(Geometric series) $\qquad S_n = \dfrac{a(1-r^n)}{1-r}$

$$\sum_{r=1}^{n} r = \frac{n(n+1)}{2}, \quad \sum_{r=1}^{n} r^2 = \frac{n(n+1)(2n+1)}{6}, \quad \sum_{r=1}^{n} r^3 = \frac{n^2(n+1)^2}{4}$$

Binomial theorem

$$(a+b)^n = \sum_{r=0}^{n} \binom{n}{r} a^{n-r}b^r \quad \text{where} \quad \binom{n}{r} = {}^nC_r = \frac{n!}{r!(n-r)!}$$

Maclaurin expansion

$$f(x) = f(0) + f'(0)x + \frac{f''(0)x^2}{2!} + \frac{f'''(0)x^3}{3!} + \frac{f^{iv}(0)x^4}{4!} + \ldots$$

De Moivre's theorem

$$[r(\cos\theta + i\sin\theta)]^n = r^n(\cos n\theta + i\sin n\theta)$$

Vector product

$$\mathbf{a}\times\mathbf{b} = |\mathbf{a}||\mathbf{b}|\sin\theta\,\hat{\mathbf{n}} = \begin{vmatrix} \mathbf{i} & \mathbf{j} & \mathbf{k} \\ a_1 & a_2 & a_3 \\ b_1 & b_2 & b_3 \end{vmatrix} = \mathbf{i}\begin{vmatrix} a_2 & a_3 \\ b_2 & b_3 \end{vmatrix} - \mathbf{j}\begin{vmatrix} a_1 & a_3 \\ b_1 & b_3 \end{vmatrix} + \mathbf{k}\begin{vmatrix} a_1 & a_2 \\ b_1 & b_2 \end{vmatrix}$$

Matrix transformation

Anti-clockwise rotation through an angle, θ about the origin, $\begin{bmatrix} \cos\theta & -\sin\theta \\ \sin\theta & \cos\theta \end{bmatrix}$

Total marks — 100

MARKS

Attempt ALL questions

1. (a) Given $f(x) = (x + 1)(x - 2)^3$, obtain the values of x for which $f'(x) = 0$. **3**

   (b) Calculate the gradient of the curve defined by $\dfrac{x^2}{y} + x = y - 5$ at the point $(3, -1)$. **4**

2. The first term of an arithmetic sequence is 2 and the 20th term is 97. Obtain the sum of the first 50 terms. **4**

3. Show that $z = 3 + 3i$ is a root of the equation $z^3 - 18z + 108 = 0$ and obtain the remaining roots of the equation. **4**

4. Let the matrix $A = \begin{pmatrix} 1 & x \\ x & 4 \end{pmatrix}$.

   (a) Obtain the value(s) of x for which A is singular. **2**

   (b) When $x = 2$, show that $A^2 = pA$ for some constant p.

   Determine the value of q such that $A^4 = qA$. **3**

5. (a) Write down the binomial expansion of $(1 + x)^5$. **1**

   (b) Hence show that 0.9^5 is 0.59049. **2**

6. Use the substitution $x = 1 + \sin\theta$ to evaluate $\displaystyle\int_0^{\frac{\pi}{2}} \dfrac{\cos\theta}{(1 + \sin\theta)^3}\, d\theta$. **5**

7. Obtain the first three non-zero terms in the Maclaurin expansion of $(1 + \sin^2 x)$. **4**

8. Prove by induction that, for all positive integers n,

$$\sum_{r=1}^{n} \frac{1}{r(r+1)} = 1 - \frac{1}{n+1}.$$

5

MARKS

9. Given that $y > -1$ and $x > -1$, obtain the general solution of the differential equation

$$\frac{dy}{dx} = 3(1+y)\sqrt{1+x},$$

expressing your answer in the form $y = f(x)$.   5

10. Use integration by parts to obtain the exact value of $\int_0^1 x\tan^{-1}x^2\, dx$.   5

11. A body moves along a straight line with velocity $v = t^3 - 12t^2 + 32t$ at time t.

(a) Obtain the value of its acceleration when $t = 0$.   1

(b) At time $t = 0$, the body is at the origin O.

Obtain a formula for the displacement of the body at time t.

Show that the body returns to O, and obtain the time, T, when this happens.   4

12. Given that $|z - 2| = |z + i|$, where $z = x + iy$, show that $ax + by + c = 0$ for suitable values of a, b and c.

Indicate on an Argand diagram the locus of complex numbers z which satisfy $|z - 2| = |z + i|$.   4

13. Prove by contradiction that if x is an irrational number, then $2 + x$ is irrational.   4

14. Obtain the general solution of the differential equation

$$\frac{d^2y}{dx^2} - 3\frac{dy}{dx} + 2y = 2x^2.$$

Given that $y = \frac{1}{2}$ and $\frac{dy}{dx} = 1$ when $x = 0$, find the particular solution.   10

15. Express $\dfrac{1}{x^3+x}$ in partial fractions.

Obtain a formula for $I(k)$, where $I(k) = \displaystyle\int_1^k \dfrac{1}{x^3+x}\,dx$, expressing it in the form $\ln\dfrac{a}{b}$, where a and b depend on k.

Write down an expression for $e^{I(k)}$ and obtain the value of $\lim_{k\to\infty} e^{I(k)}$.   **10**

16. Let $f(x) = \dfrac{x}{\ln x}$ for $x > 1$.

  (a) Derive expressions for $f'(x)$ and $f''(x)$, simplifying your answers.   **4**

  (b) Obtain the coordinates and nature of the stationary point of the curve $y = f(x)$.   **3**

  (c) Obtain the coordinates of the point of inflexion.   **2**

17.   (a) Use Gaussian elimination on the following system of equations to give an expression for z in terms of λ.

$$x + y - z = 6$$
$$2x - 3y + 2z = 2$$
$$-5x + 2y + \lambda z = 1$$

     Determine the solution to this system of equations when $\lambda = -4$.   **5**

  (b) Show that the line of intersection, L, of the planes $x + y - z = 6$ and $2x - 3y + 2z = 2$ has parametric equations

$$x = t$$
$$y = 4t - 14$$
$$z = 5t - 20.$$ **2**

  (c) Find the acute angle between line L and the plane $-5x + 2y - 4z = 1$.   **4**

[END OF MODEL PAPER]

ADVANCED HIGHER

2016

National
Qualifications
2016

X747/77/11   **Mathematics**

THURSDAY, 12 MAY

9:00 AM — 12:00 NOON

Total marks — 100

Attempt ALL questions.

You may use a calculator.

Full credit will be given only to solutions which contain appropriate working.

State the units for your answer where appropriate.

Answers obtained by readings from scale drawings will not receive any credit.

Write your answers clearly in the answer booklet provided. In the answer booklet, you must clearly identify the question number you are attempting.

Use **blue** or **black** ink.

Before leaving the examination room you must give your answer booklet to the Invigilator; if you do not, you may lose all the marks for this paper.

FORMULAE LIST

Standard derivatives	
$f(x)$	$f'(x)$
$\sin^{-1} x$	$\dfrac{1}{\sqrt{1-x^2}}$
$\cos^{-1} x$	$-\dfrac{1}{\sqrt{1-x^2}}$
$\tan^{-1} x$	$\dfrac{1}{1+x^2}$
$\tan x$	$\sec^2 x$
$\cot x$	$-\operatorname{cosec}^2 x$
$\sec x$	$\sec x \tan x$
$\operatorname{cosec} x$	$-\operatorname{cosec} x \cot x$
$\ln x$	$\dfrac{1}{x}$
e^x	e^x

Standard integrals	
$f(x)$	$\int f(x)\,dx$
$\sec^2(ax)$	$\dfrac{1}{a}\tan(ax)+c$
$\dfrac{1}{\sqrt{a^2-x^2}}$	$\sin^{-1}\left(\dfrac{x}{a}\right)+c$
$\dfrac{1}{a^2+x^2}$	$\dfrac{1}{a}\tan^{-1}\left(\dfrac{x}{a}\right)+c$
$\dfrac{1}{x}$	$\ln|x|+c$
e^{ax}	$\dfrac{1}{a}e^{ax}+c$

Summations

(Arithmetic series) $S_n = \dfrac{1}{2}n\left[2a+(n-1)d\right]$

(Geometric series) $S_n = \dfrac{a\left(1-r^n\right)}{1-r}$

$$\sum_{r=1}^{n} r = \frac{n(n+1)}{2}, \quad \sum_{r=1}^{n} r^2 = \frac{n(n+1)(2n+1)}{6}, \quad \sum_{r=1}^{n} r^3 = \frac{n^2(n+1)^2}{4}$$

Binomial theorem

$$(a+b)^n = \sum_{r=0}^{n} \binom{n}{r} a^{n-r} b^r \quad \text{where} \quad \binom{n}{r} = {}^nC_r = \frac{n!}{r!(n-r)!}$$

Maclaurin expansion

$$f(x) = f(0) + f'(0)x + \frac{f''(0)x^2}{2!} + \frac{f'''(0)x^3}{3!} + \frac{f^{iv}(0)x^4}{4!} + \dots$$

FORMULAE LIST (continued)

De Moivre's theorem

$$[r(\cos\theta + i\sin\theta)]^n = r^n(\cos n\theta + i\sin n\theta)$$

Vector product

$$\mathbf{a}\times\mathbf{b} = |\mathbf{a}||\mathbf{b}|\sin\theta\,\hat{\mathbf{n}} = \begin{vmatrix} \mathbf{i} & \mathbf{j} & \mathbf{k} \\ a_1 & a_2 & a_3 \\ b_1 & b_2 & b_3 \end{vmatrix} = \mathbf{i}\begin{vmatrix} a_2 & a_3 \\ b_2 & b_3 \end{vmatrix} - \mathbf{j}\begin{vmatrix} a_1 & a_3 \\ b_1 & b_3 \end{vmatrix} + \mathbf{k}\begin{vmatrix} a_1 & a_2 \\ b_1 & b_2 \end{vmatrix}$$

Matrix transformation

Anti-clockwise rotation through an angle, θ, about the origin, $\begin{bmatrix} \cos\theta & -\sin\theta \\ \sin\theta & \cos\theta \end{bmatrix}$

[Turn over

Total marks — 100

Attempt ALL questions

1. (a) Differentiate $y = x\tan^{-1}2x$. **3**

   (b) Given $f(x) = \dfrac{1-x^2}{1+4x^2}$, find $f'(x)$, simplifying your answer. **3**

   (c) A curve is given by the parametric equations

   $$x = 6t \text{ and } y = 1 - \cos t.$$

   Find $\dfrac{dy}{dx}$ in terms of t. **2**

2. A geometric sequence has second and fifth terms 108 and 4 respectively.

   (a) Calculate the value of the common ratio. **3**

   (b) State why the associated geometric series has a sum to infinity. **1**

   (c) Find the value of this sum to infinity. **2**

3. Write down and simplify the general term in the binomial expansion of $\left(\dfrac{3}{x} - 2x\right)^{13}$.

   Hence, or otherwise, find the term in x^9. **5**

4. Below is a system of equations:

   $$x + 2y + 3z = 3$$
   $$2x - y + 4z = 5$$
   $$x - 3y + 2\lambda z = 2$$

   Use Gaussian elimination to find the value of λ which leads to redundancy. **4**

5. Prove **by induction** that

   $$\sum_{r=1}^{n} r(3r-1) = n^2(n+1), \qquad \forall n \in \mathbb{N}.$$ **4**

MARKS

6. Find Maclaurin expansions for $\sin 3x$ and e^{4x} up to and including the term in x^3.

   Hence obtain an expansion for $e^{4x}\sin 3x$ up to and including the term in x^3.   **6**

7. A is the matrix $\begin{pmatrix} 2 & 0 \\ \lambda & -1 \end{pmatrix}$.

   (a) Find the determinant of matrix A.   **1**

   (b) Show that A^2 can be expressed in the form $pA+qI$, stating the values of p and q.   **3**

   (c) Obtain a similar expression for A^4.   **2**

8. Let $z = \sqrt{3} - i$.

   (a) Plot z on an Argand diagram.   **1**

   (b) Let $w = az$ where $a > 0$, $a \in \mathbb{R}$.

   Express w in polar form.   **2**

   (c) Express w^8 in the form $ka^n\left(x + i\sqrt{y}\right)$ where $k, x, y \in \mathbb{Z}$.   **3**

9. Obtain $\int x^7 \left(\ln x\right)^2 dx$.   **6**

10. For each of the following statements, decide whether it is true or false.

    If true, give a proof; if false, give a counterexample.

    A. If a positive integer p is prime, then so is $2p+1$.

    B. If a positive integer n has remainder 1 when divided by 3, then n^3 also has remainder 1 when divided by 3.   **4**

11. The height of a cube is increasing at the rate of $5\,\text{cm}\,\text{s}^{-1}$.

    Find the rate of increase of the volume when the height of the cube is $3\,\text{cm}$.   **4**

[Turn over

[BLANK PAGE]

DO NOT WRITE ON THIS PAGE

ADVANCED HIGHER

2017

National
Qualifications
2017

X747/77/11

Mathematics

FRIDAY, 5 MAY

9:00 AM — 12:00 NOON

Total marks — 100

Attempt ALL questions.

You may use a calculator.

Full credit will be given only to solutions which contain appropriate working.

State the units for your answer where appropriate.

Answers obtained by readings from scale drawings will not receive any credit.

Write your answers clearly in the answer booklet provided. In the answer booklet, you must clearly identify the question number you are attempting.

Use **blue** or **black** ink.

Before leaving the examination room you must give your answer booklet to the Invigilator; if you do not, you may lose all the marks for this paper.

FORMULAE LIST

Standard derivatives	
$f(x)$	$f'(x)$
$\sin^{-1}x$	$\dfrac{1}{\sqrt{1-x^2}}$
$\cos^{-1}x$	$-\dfrac{1}{\sqrt{1-x^2}}$
$\tan^{-1}x$	$\dfrac{1}{1+x^2}$
$\tan x$	$\sec^2 x$
$\cot x$	$-\operatorname{cosec}^2 x$
$\sec x$	$\sec x \tan x$
$\operatorname{cosec} x$	$-\operatorname{cosec} x \cot x$
$\ln x$	$\dfrac{1}{x}$
e^x	e^x

Standard integrals	
$f(x)$	$\int f(x)\,dx$
$\sec^2(ax)$	$\dfrac{1}{a}\tan(ax)+c$
$\dfrac{1}{\sqrt{a^2-x^2}}$	$\sin^{-1}\left(\dfrac{x}{a}\right)+c$
$\dfrac{1}{a^2+x^2}$	$\dfrac{1}{a}\tan^{-1}\left(\dfrac{x}{a}\right)+c$
$\dfrac{1}{x}$	$\ln|x|+c$
e^{ax}	$\dfrac{1}{a}e^{ax}+c$

Summations

(Arithmetic series) $\qquad S_n = \dfrac{1}{2}n\left[2a+(n-1)d\right]$

(Geometric series) $\qquad S_n = \dfrac{a(1-r^n)}{1-r}$

$$\sum_{r=1}^{n} r = \frac{n(n+1)}{2}, \quad \sum_{r=1}^{n} r^2 = \frac{n(n+1)(2n+1)}{6}, \quad \sum_{r=1}^{n} r^3 = \frac{n^2(n+1)^2}{4}$$

Binomial theorem

$$(a+b)^n = \sum_{r=0}^{n} \binom{n}{r} a^{n-r}b^r \quad \text{where} \quad \binom{n}{r} = {}^nC_r = \frac{n!}{r!(n-r)!}$$

Maclaurin expansion

$$f(x) = f(0) + f'(0)x + \frac{f''(0)x^2}{2!} + \frac{f'''(0)x^3}{3!} + \frac{f^{iv}(0)x^4}{4!} + \dots$$

FORMULAE LIST (continued)

De Moivre's theorem

$$\left[r(\cos\theta + i\sin\theta)\right]^n = r^n\left(\cos n\theta + i\sin n\theta\right)$$

Vector product

$$\mathbf{a}\times\mathbf{b} = |\mathbf{a}||\mathbf{b}|\sin\theta\,\hat{\mathbf{n}} = \begin{vmatrix} \mathbf{i} & \mathbf{j} & \mathbf{k} \\ a_1 & a_2 & a_3 \\ b_1 & b_2 & b_3 \end{vmatrix} = \mathbf{i}\begin{vmatrix} a_2 & a_3 \\ b_2 & b_3 \end{vmatrix} - \mathbf{j}\begin{vmatrix} a_1 & a_3 \\ b_1 & b_3 \end{vmatrix} + \mathbf{k}\begin{vmatrix} a_1 & a_2 \\ b_1 & b_2 \end{vmatrix}$$

Matrix transformation

Anti-clockwise rotation through an angle, θ, about the origin, $\begin{bmatrix} \cos\theta & -\sin\theta \\ \sin\theta & \cos\theta \end{bmatrix}$

[Turn over

Total marks — 100

MARKS

Attempt ALL questions

1. Write down the binomial expansion of $\left(\dfrac{2}{y^2} - 5y\right)^3$ and simplify your answer.

   4

2. Express $\dfrac{x^2 - 6x + 20}{(x+1)(x-2)^2}$ in partial fractions.

   4

3. On a suitable domain, a function is defined by $f(x) = \dfrac{e^{x^2 - 1}}{x^2 - 1}$.

   Find $f'(x)$, simplifying your answer.

   3

4. The fifth term of an arithmetic sequence is −6 and the twelfth term is −34.

   (a) Determine the values of the first term and the common difference.

   2

   (b) Obtain algebraically the value of n for which $S_n = -144$.

   3

5. (a)   (i)   Use Gaussian elimination on the system of equations below to give an expression for z in terms of λ.

   4

$$x + 2y - z = -3$$
$$4x - 2y + 3z = 11$$
$$3x + y + 2\lambda z = 8$$

        (ii)   For what value of λ is this system of equations inconsistent?

   1

   (b) Determine the solution of this system when $\lambda = -2 \cdot 5$.

   1

6. Use the substitution $u = 5x^2$ to find the exact value of $\displaystyle\int_{0}^{\frac{1}{\sqrt{10}}} \dfrac{x}{\sqrt{1 - 25x^4}}\,dx$.

   6

MARKS

7. Matrices P and Q are defined by $P = \begin{pmatrix} x & 2 \\ -5 & -1 \end{pmatrix}$ and $Q = \begin{pmatrix} 2 & -3 \\ 4 & y \end{pmatrix}$, where $x, y \in \mathbb{R}$.

    (a) Given the determinant of P is 2, obtain:

        (i) The value of x.   1

        (ii) P^{-1}.   1

        (iii) $P^{-1}Q'$, where Q' is the transpose of Q.   2

    (b) The matrix R is defined by $R = \begin{pmatrix} 5 & -2 \\ z & -6 \end{pmatrix}$, where $z \in \mathbb{R}$.

    Determine the value of z such that R is singular.   2

8. Use the Euclidean algorithm to find integers a and b such that $1595a + 1218b = 29$.   4

9. Solve $\dfrac{dy}{dx} = e^{2x}\left(1 + y^2\right)$ given that when $x = 0$, $y = 1$.

Express y in terms of x.   5

10. S_n is defined by $\displaystyle\sum_{r=1}^{n}\left(r^2 + \frac{1}{3}r\right)$.

    (a) Find an expression for S_n, fully factorising your answer.   2

    (b) Hence find an expression for $\displaystyle\sum_{r=10}^{2p}\left(r^2 + \frac{1}{3}r\right)$ where $p > 5$.   2

[Turn over

MARKS

11. Given $y = x^{2x^3+1}$, use logarithmic differentiation to find $\dfrac{dy}{dx}$.

Write your answer in terms of x.

5

12. In the diagram below part of the graph of $y = f(x)$ has been omitted.

The point $(-1, -2)$ lies on the graph and the line $y = \dfrac{1}{2}x - 3$ is an asymptote.

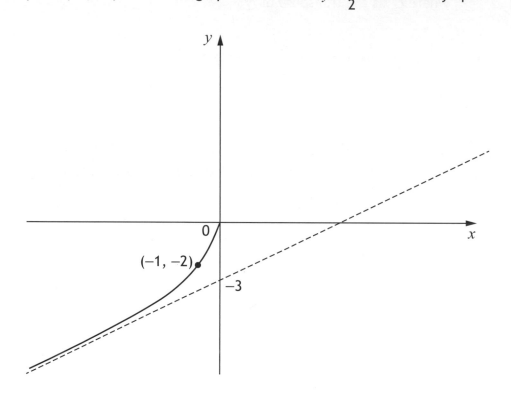

Given that $f(x)$ is an odd function:

(a) Copy and complete the diagram, including any asymptotes and any points you know to be on the graph.

2

(b) $g(x) = |f(x)|$. On a separate diagram, sketch $g(x)$.

Include known asymptotes and points.

2

(c) State the range of values of $f'(x)$ given that $f'(0) = 2$.

1

13. Let n be an integer.

Using proof by contrapositive, show that if n^2 is even, then n is even.

4

MARKS

14. Find the particular solution of the differential equation

$$\frac{d^2y}{dx^2} - 6\frac{dy}{dx} + 9y = 8\sin x + 19\cos x$$

given that $y = 7$ and $\frac{dy}{dx} = \frac{1}{2}$ when $x = 0$.   10

15. (a) A beam of light passes through the points B(7, 8, 1) and T(−3, −22, 6).

Obtain parametric equations of the line representing the beam of light.   2

(b) A sheet of metal is represented by a plane containing the points P(2, 1, 9), Q(1, 2, 7) and R(−3, 7, 1).

Find the Cartesian equation of the plane.   4

(c) The beam of light passes through a hole in the metal at point H.

Find the coordinates of H.   3

16. On a suitable domain, a curve is defined by the equation $4x^2 + 9y^2 = 36$.

A section of the curve in the first quadrant, illustrated in the diagram below, is rotated 360° about the **y-axis**.

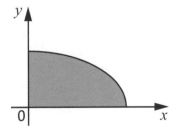

Calculate the exact value of the volume generated.   5

[Turn over for next question

17. The complex number $z = 2 + i$ is a root of the polynomial equation $z^4 - 6z^3 + 16z^2 - 22z + q = 0$, where $q \in \mathbb{Z}$.

MARKS

(a) State a second root of the equation.

1

(b) Find the value of q and the remaining roots.

6

(c) Show the solutions to $z^4 - 6z^3 + 16z^2 - 22z + q = 0$ on an Argand diagram.

1

18. The position of a particle at time t is given by the parametric equations

$x = t \cos t, \quad y = t \sin t, \quad t \geq 0.$

(a) Find an expression for the instantaneous speed of the particle.

5

The diagram below shows the path that the particle takes.

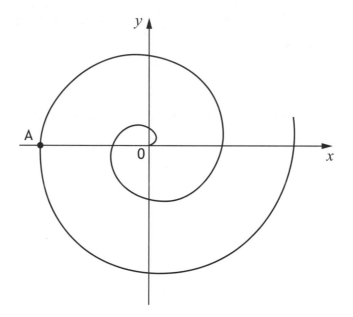

(b) Calculate the instantaneous speed of the particle at point A.

2

[END OF QUESTION PAPER]

ADVANCED HIGHER

Answers

ADVANCED HIGHER MATHEMATICS
2015 SPECIMEN QUESTION PAPER

Question			Expected response (Give one mark for each •)	Max mark	Additional guidance (Illustration of evidence for awarding a mark at each •)
1.			Ans: demonstrate result •1 know and start to use quotient rule •2 complete differentiation •3 simplify numerator	3	•1 $\dfrac{(1+x^2)\times 1 - \ldots}{(1-x^2)^2}$ •2 $\dfrac{(1+x^2)\times 1 - 2x(x-1)}{(1+x^2)^2}$ •3 $\dfrac{1+x^2-2x^2+2x}{(1+x^2)^2} = \dfrac{1+2x-x^2}{(1+x^2)^2}$
2.			Ans: 6000 •1 correct substitution into general term •2 simplify •3 identify r and find coefficient	3	•1 $\dbinom{6}{r}(2x)^{6-r}\left(-\dfrac{5}{x^2}\right)^r$ •2 $\dbinom{6}{2}2^{6-r}(-5)^r x^{6-3r}$ •3 $\dbinom{6}{2}(2)^4(-5)^2 = 6000$

Notes:

1. Accept $\dbinom{6}{6-r}(2x)^{6-r}\left(-\dfrac{5}{x^2}\right)^r$ or correct equivalent for •1.
2. If coefficient is found by expanding the expression, only •3 is available.

| 3. | | | Ans: $\dfrac{1}{2}\sin^{-1}\left(\dfrac{4x}{3}\right)+c$
 •1 evidence of identifying an appropiate method

 •2 re-write in standard form

 •3 final answer with constant of integration | 3 | •1 e.g. identify standard integral
 $\displaystyle\int \dfrac{1}{\sqrt{a^2-x^2}}\,dx$

 •2 $2\displaystyle\int \dfrac{1}{4\sqrt{\left(\dfrac{3}{4}\right)^2-x^2}}\,dx$ or equivalent

 •3 $2\times\dfrac{1}{4}\sin^{-1}\left(\dfrac{4x}{3}\right)+c = \dfrac{1}{2}\sin^{-1}\left(\dfrac{4x}{3}\right)+c$ |

Note:
For •1 accept any appropriate evidence e.g. using substitution $u = 4x$.

Question	Expected response (Give one mark for each •)	Max mark	Additional guidance (Illustration of evidence for awarding a mark at each •)
4.	Ans: $x = 244, y = -163$	4	
	•^{1} start correctly		•^{1} $729 = 487 \times 1 + 242$
	•^{2} show last non–zero remainder $= 1$		•^{2} $487 = 242 \times 2 + 3$ $242 = 80 \times 3 + 2$ $3 = 2 \times 1 + 1$ $2 = 2 \times 1 + 0, \qquad GCD = 1$
	•^{3} evidence of two correct back substitutions using $2 = 242 - 3 \times 80$ or $3 = 487 - 242 \times 2$ or $242 = 729 - 487 \times 1$		•^{3} $1 = 3 - 2 \times 1 = 3 - (242 - 80 \times 3) = 81 \times 3 - 242$ $\quad = 81(487 - 2 \times 242) - 242$ $\quad = 81 \times 487 - 163 \times 242$ $\quad = 81 \times 487 - 163(729 - 487)$ $\quad = 244 \times 487 - 163 \times 729$ carefully check for equivalent alternatives
	•^{4} values for x and y		•^{4} $1 = 487 \times 244 - 729 \times 163$ So, $x = 244, y = -163$
5.	Ans: $\dfrac{x^2 e^{3x}}{3} - \dfrac{2xe^{3x}}{9} + \dfrac{2e^{3x}}{27} + c$	5	
	•^{1} evidence of application of integration by parts		•^{1} $\left(x^2 \int e^{3x}\, dx - \int \left(\int e^{3x} \cdot \dfrac{d}{dx} x^2\, dx \right) dx \right)$
	•^{2} correct choice of u and v'		•^{2} $u = x^2 \ v' = e^{3x}$
	•^{3} correct first application		•^{3} $\dfrac{1}{3} x^2 e^{3x} - \dfrac{2}{3} \int xe^{3x}\, dx$ or equivalent
	•^{4} start second application		•^{4} $\int xe^{3x}\, dx = \dfrac{xe^{3x}}{3} - \dfrac{e^{3x}}{9}$ or equivalent
	•^{5} final answer with constant of integration		•^{5} $\dfrac{x^2 e^{3x}}{3} - \dfrac{2xe^{3x}}{9} + \dfrac{2e^{3x}}{27} + c$ or equivalent
6.	Ans: $k = \dfrac{3}{2}, -4$	4	
	•^{1} starts process for working out determinant		•^{1} $3 \begin{vmatrix} -4 & 2 \\ 0 & 1 \end{vmatrix} - k \begin{vmatrix} 3 & 2 \\ k & 1 \end{vmatrix} + 2 \begin{vmatrix} 3 & -4 \\ k & 0 \end{vmatrix}$
	•^{2} completing process correctly		•^{2} $-12 - k(3 - 2k) + 8k$
	•^{3} simplify and equate to 0		•^{3} $2k^2 + 5k - 12 = 0$
	•^{4} find values of k		•^{4} $k = \dfrac{3}{2}, \quad k = -4$

Note:
Accept answer arrived at through row and column operations.

Question			Expected response (Give one mark for each •)	Max mark	Additional guidance (Illustration of evidence for awarding a mark at each •)
7.			Ans: $\dfrac{dV}{dt} = 600\,\pi\,\text{cm}^3\text{s}^{-1}$	5	
			•^{1} interprets rate of change		•^{1} $\dfrac{dA}{dt} = \dfrac{dA}{dr} \times \dfrac{dr}{dt} = 120\pi$
			•^{2} correct expression for $\dfrac{dA}{dr}$		•^{2} $A = 4\pi r^2,\ \dfrac{dA}{dr} = 8\pi r$
			•^{3} find $\dfrac{dr}{dt}$		•^{3} $\dfrac{dr}{dt} = \dfrac{120\pi}{80\pi} = \dfrac{3}{2}$
			•^{4} correct expression for $\dfrac{dV}{dt}$		•^{4} $\dfrac{dV}{dt} = \dfrac{dV}{dr} \times \dfrac{dr}{dt} = 4\pi r^2 \times \dfrac{3}{2}$
			•^{5} evaluates $\dfrac{dV}{dt}$		•^{5} $\dfrac{dV}{dt} = 4\pi(10)^2 \times \dfrac{3}{2} = 600\,\pi\,\text{cm}^3\,\text{s}^{-1}$
8.	(a)	(i)	Ans: $f(x) = 1 + 3x + \dfrac{9}{2}x^2 + \dfrac{9}{2}x^3 + \ldots$	2	
			•^{1} state Maclaurin expansion for e^{3x} up to e^3		•^{1} $f(x) = 1 + \dfrac{3x}{1!} + \dfrac{(3x)^2}{2!} + \dfrac{(3x)^3}{3!} + \ldots$
			•^{2} correct expansion		•^{2} $f(x) = 1 + 3x + \dfrac{9}{2}x^2 + \dfrac{9}{2}x^3 + \ldots$
		(ii)	Ans: $g(x) = \dfrac{1}{4} - \dfrac{1}{4}x + \dfrac{3}{16}x^2 - \dfrac{1}{8}x^3 + \ldots$	3	
			•^{3} correct differentiation of $g(x)$		•^{3} $g(x) = (x+2)^{-2},\ g'(x) = -2(x+2)^{-3},$ $g''(x) = 6(x+2)^{-4},\ g'''(x) = -24(x+2)^{-5}$
			•^{4} correct evaluations of g functions		•^{4} $g(0) = \dfrac{1}{4},\ g'(0) = -\dfrac{1}{4},\ g''(0) = \dfrac{3}{8}$ $g'''(0) = -\dfrac{3}{4}$
			•^{5} correct expansion		•^{5} $g(x) = \dfrac{1}{4} - \dfrac{1}{4}x + \dfrac{3}{16}x^2 - \dfrac{1}{8}x^3 + \ldots$
	(b)		Ans: $h\!\left(\dfrac{1}{2}\right) = 0 \cdot 327$	3	
			•^{6} connection between $h(x),\,f(x)$ and $g(x)$		•^{6} $h(x) = x\,f(x)g(x)$
			•^{7} approximate $f\!\left(\dfrac{1}{2}\right)$ and $g\!\left(\dfrac{1}{2}\right)$		•^{7} $f\!\left(\dfrac{1}{2}\right) = 4 \cdot 1875,\ g\!\left(\dfrac{1}{2}\right) = 0 \cdot 15625$
			•^{8} evaluate $h\!\left(\dfrac{1}{2}\right)$		•^{8} $h\!\left(\dfrac{1}{2}\right) = 0 \cdot 327$

Note:
Accept answer given as a fraction.
For (a) (ii) award full credit for answers arrived at using a binomial expansion.
For (b) evidence of use of the expansions from (a) must be evident. Candidates who simply calculate the value of $h\!\left(\frac{1}{2}\right)$ directly without using the approximations from (a) receive no marks for (b).

Question	Expected response (Give one mark for each •)	Max mark	Additional guidance (Illustration of evidence for awarding a mark at each •)

9.	Ans: proof, $r = \dfrac{9}{4}$
	
	 •^{1} create term formulae
	
	 •^{2} form ratios for r
	
	 •^{3} complete proof
	
	 •^{4} evaluate r
		4	•^{1} $u_3 = a + 2d$
			     $u_7 = a + 6d$
			     $u_{16} = a + 15d$
			
			 •^{2} $\dfrac{a+15d}{a+6d} = \dfrac{a+6d}{a+2d}$
			
			 •^{3} $(a+15d)(a+2d) = (a+6d)^2$
			     $a^2 + 17ad + 30d^2 = a^2 + 12ad + 36d^2$
			     $5a = 6d$
			     $a = \dfrac{6}{5}d$
			
			 •^{4} $r = \dfrac{\frac{6}{5}d + 6d}{\frac{6}{5}d + 2d} = \dfrac{9}{4}$

10.	Ans: $\dfrac{dy}{dx} = \dfrac{3}{3x+2} + 2 - \dfrac{4}{2x-1}$ •^{1} introduction of $\log_e$ •^{2} express function in differentiable form •^{3} differentiate	3	•^{1} $y = \ln\left(\dfrac{(3x+2)\,e^{2x}}{(2x-1)^2} \right)$ •^{2} $y = \ln|3x+2| + 2x - 2\ln|2x-1|$ •^{3} $\dfrac{dy}{dx} = \dfrac{3}{3x+2} + 2 - \dfrac{4}{2x-1}$

Note:
In this question the use of modulus signs is not required for the award of •^{1} and •^{2}.

Question	Expected response (Give one mark for each •)	Max mark	Additional guidance (Illustration of evidence for awarding a mark at each •)

11.	Ans: $\ln 2 - \dfrac{1}{6}$
	
	 •^{1} correct form of partial fractions
	 •^{2} 1st coefficient correct
	 •^{3} 2nd coefficient correct
	 •^{4} 3rd coefficient correct
	
	 •^{5} •^{6} integrate any two terms
	      integrate all three terms
	
	 •^{7} evaluate
		7	•^{1} $\dfrac{A}{x+1} + \dfrac{B}{(x+1)^2} + \dfrac{C}{2x-1}$
			
			 •^{2} $A = -1$
			 •^{3} $B = -1$
			 •^{4} $C = 2$
			
			 •^{5} •^{6} $\displaystyle\int_1^2 \left(\dfrac{2}{2x-1} - \dfrac{1}{x+1} - \dfrac{1}{(x+1)^2} \right) dx$
			
			     $= \left[\ln|2x-1| - \ln|x+1| + (x+1)^{-1} \right]_1^2$
			
			 •^{7} $\ln 2 - \dfrac{1}{6}$

Note:
Do not penalise the omission of the modulus signs at •^{5} and •^{6}.

Question			Expected response (Give one mark for each •)	Max mark	Additional guidance (Illustration of evidence for awarding a mark at each •)
12.	(a)		Ans: m is odd and n is odd •¹ correct statement	1	•¹ m is odd and n is odd
	(b)		Ans: proof •² contrapositive statement •³ begin proof •⁴ complete proof	3	•² If m and n are both odd then mn is odd. •³ Let $m = 2p - 1$, $n = 2q - 1$ where p, q are positive integers. Then, $mn = 2(2pq - p - q) + 1$ where $2pq - p - q$ is clearly an integer therefore mn is clearly odd. •⁴ And so the contrapositive statement is true and it follows that the original statement, 'if mn is even then m is even or n is even', that is equivalent to the contrapositive, is true.

Note:
For •¹ accept an equivalent statement, e.g. **'neither m nor n is even'** but do not accept any other answer, e.g. 'It is not true to say that m is even or n is even'.

Question			Expected response	Max mark	Additional guidance
13.	(a)		Ans: $x = 4$, $x = -2$ with explanation •¹ correct asymptotes •² suitable explanation	2	•¹ $x^2 - 2x - 8 = 0 \Leftrightarrow x = 4$ or $x = -2$ •² y tends towards $\pm\infty$ as $x \to 4$ and $x \to -2$
	(b)	(i)	Ans: false with explanation •³ suitable explanation	1	•³ The statement is false because the graph meets the x–axis when $x = \dfrac{3}{4}$.
		(ii)	Ans: proof •⁴ method •⁵ complete proof	2	•⁴ e.g. $f(x) = \dfrac{\dfrac{4}{x} - \dfrac{3}{x^2}}{1 - \dfrac{2}{x} - \dfrac{8}{x^2}}$ •⁵ As $x \to \pm\infty$, $f(x) \to \dfrac{0}{1} = 0$ i.e. the line $y = 0$ is a horizontal asymptote

Note:
For •² accept $4x - 3 \neq 0$ at $x = 4$ or $x = -2$.

Question			Expected response	Max mark	Additional guidance
14.	(a)		Ans: $(3, -2, 8)$ •¹ write lines in parametric form •² create equations for intersection •³ solve a pair of these equations (e.g. the first two) for p and t •⁴ check that the third equation is satisfied •⁵ state coordinates of point of intersection	5	•¹ $\begin{array}{ll} x = 3t - 6 & x = 4p - 5 \\ y = -t + 1 & \text{and} \quad y = p - 4 \\ z = 2t + 2 & z = 4p \end{array}$ •² $\begin{array}{l} 4p - 5 = 3t - 6 \\ p - 4 = -t + 1 \\ 4p = 2t + 2 \end{array}$ •³ $t = 3$ and $p = 2$ •⁴ e.g. $4(2) = 2(3) + 2$ •⁵ evidence of substitution into third equation and $(3, -2, 8)$

Question		Expected response (Give one mark for each •)	Max mark	Additional guidance (Illustration of evidence for awarding a mark at each •)
	(b)	Ans: $-6x - 4y + 7z = 46$ •6 use vector product to find normal to the plane •7 evaluate normal vector •8 form equation of plane	3	•6 $\begin{vmatrix} \mathbf{i} & \mathbf{j} & \mathbf{k} \\ 3 & -1 & 2 \\ 4 & 1 & 4 \end{vmatrix}$ •7 $-6\mathbf{i} - 4\mathbf{j} + 7\mathbf{k}$ •8 $-6x - 4y + 7z = 46$
	(c)	Ans: $49°$ •9 select correct vectors •10 complete calculations of $\lvert a \rvert$, $\lvert b \rvert$ and $a \cdot b$ •11 evaluate acute angle between normal to plane and line •12 calculate angle between line and plane	4	•9 $\begin{pmatrix} -6 \\ -4 \\ 7 \end{pmatrix}$ and $\begin{pmatrix} 2 \\ 4 \\ -1 \end{pmatrix}$ •10 $\left\lVert \begin{pmatrix} -6 \\ -4 \\ 7 \end{pmatrix} \right\rVert = \sqrt{101}$, $\left\lVert \begin{pmatrix} 2 \\ 4 \\ -1 \end{pmatrix} \right\rVert = \sqrt{21}$ and $\begin{pmatrix} -6 \\ -4 \\ 7 \end{pmatrix} \cdot \begin{pmatrix} 2 \\ 4 \\ -1 \end{pmatrix} = -35$ •11 $40\cdot54°$ •12 $90° - 40\cdot54° = 49\cdot46°$
15.	(a)	Ans: $\dfrac{2}{(1-x^2)}$ •1 express function in differentiable form •2 complete process	2	•1 $\ln(1+x) - \ln(1-x)$ •2 $\dfrac{1}{1+x} + \dfrac{1}{1-x} = \dfrac{2}{(1-x^2)}$
	(b)	Ans: $y = \dfrac{x + e - 2\pi}{e^{\sec x}}$ •3 express in standard form •4 form of integrating factor •5 find integrating factor •6 state modified equation •7 integrate both sides •8 substitute in for x and y and find c •9 state particular solution	7	•3 $\dfrac{dy}{dx} + y\dfrac{\tan x}{\cos x} = \dfrac{1}{e^{\sec x}}$ •4 $\text{IF} = e^{\int \frac{\tan x}{\cos x}\,dx}$ •5 $\text{IF} = e^{\sec x}$ •6 $\dfrac{d}{dx}(ye^{\sec x}) = 1$ •7 $e^{\sec x}y = x + c$ •8 $e^{\sec 2\pi} \cdot 1 = 2\pi + c$, $c = e - 2\pi$ •9 $y = \dfrac{x + e - 2\pi}{e^{\sec x}}$

Question			Expected response (Give one mark for each •)	Max mark	Additional guidance (Illustration of evidence for awarding a mark at each •)
16.	(a)		Ans: proof	5	
			•¹ strategy use partial fractions		•¹ $\dfrac{1}{r(r+1)} = \dfrac{A}{r} + \dfrac{B}{r+1}$
			•² find A and B		•² $A = 1, B = -1$
			•³ state result and start to write out series		•³ $1 - \dfrac{1}{2} + \dfrac{1}{2} - \dfrac{1}{3} + \dfrac{1}{3} - \dfrac{1}{4} + \dfrac{1}{4} - \dfrac{1}{5} \cdots$ $+ \dfrac{1}{n-1} - \dfrac{1}{n} + \dfrac{1}{n} - \dfrac{1}{n+1}$
			•⁴ strategy		•⁴ Note that successive terms cancel out (telescopic series) $1 + \left(-\dfrac{1}{2} + \dfrac{1}{2}\right) + \left(-\dfrac{1}{3} + \dfrac{1}{3}\right) + \left(-\dfrac{1}{4} + \dfrac{1}{4}\right)$ $+ \left(-\dfrac{1}{5} + \cdots\right) + \left(\cdots + \dfrac{1}{n-1}\right) + \left(-\dfrac{1}{n} + \dfrac{1}{n}\right) - \dfrac{1}{n+1}$
			•⁵ complete proof		•⁵ cancels terms and $1 - \dfrac{1}{n+1} = \dfrac{n}{n+1}$
	(a)		Ans: proof (alternative)		
			•¹ state hypothesis and consider $n = k+1$		•¹ Assume $\displaystyle\sum_{r=1}^{k} \dfrac{1}{r(r+1)} = \dfrac{k}{k+1}$ true for some $n = k$, **and** consider $n = k+1$ i.e. $\displaystyle\sum_{r=1}^{k+1} \dfrac{1}{r(r+1)} = \sum_{r=1}^{k} \dfrac{1}{r(r+1)} + \dfrac{1}{(k+1)(k+2)}$
			•² start process for $k+1$		•² $\dfrac{k}{k+1} + \dfrac{1}{(k+1)(k+2)}$ $= \dfrac{k(k+2)}{(k+1)(k+2)} + \dfrac{1}{(k+1)(k+2)}$ $= \dfrac{k^2 + 2k + 1}{(k+1)(k+2)}$
			•³ complete process		•³ $= \dfrac{(k+1)^2}{(k+1)(k+2)}$ $\dfrac{(k+1)}{(k+1)+1}$
			•⁴ show true for $n = 1$		•⁴ For $n = 1$ LHS $= \dfrac{1}{1(1+1)} = \dfrac{1}{2}$ RHS $= \dfrac{1}{1+1} = \dfrac{1}{2}$ LHS = RHS so true for $n = 1$
			•⁵ state conclusion		•⁵ Hence, if true for $n = k$, then true for $n = k+1$, but since true for $n = 1$, then by induction true for all positive integers n.

Question			Expected response (Give one mark for each •)	Max mark	Additional guidance (Illustration of evidence for awarding a mark at each •)
(b)	(i)		Ans: $n = 31$	3	
			•^{6} set up equation and start to solve		•^{6} e.g. $\dfrac{n+1}{n+2} - \dfrac{n}{n+1} < \dfrac{1}{1000}$ and evidence of strategy
			•^{7} process		•^{7} $n^2 + 3n - 998 > 0$
			•^{8} obtain solution		•^{8} $n = 31$
	(ii)		Ans: $n = 11$	2	
			•^{9} set up equation		•^{9} $\left(\dfrac{n}{n+1}\right)\left(\dfrac{n-1}{n}\right)\left(\dfrac{n-2}{n-1}\right) = \dfrac{n-8}{n-7}$
			•^{10} solve for n		•^{10} $n = 11$

Notes:
1. •^{1} is only available for induction hypothesis and stating that $k + 1$ is going to be considered.
2. •^{3} is only awarded if final line shows results required in terms of $k + 1$ and is arrived at by appropriate working, including target/desired result approach, from the •^{3} stage.
3. •^{5} is only awarded if the candidate shows clear understanding of the logic required.

Question		Expected response (Give one mark for each •)	Max mark	Additional guidance (Illustration of evidence for awarding a mark at each •)
17.	(a)	Ans: proof	5	
		•^{1} use de Moivre's theorem		•^{1} $z^4 = \cos 4\theta + i \sin 4\theta$
		•^{2} start process using binomial theorem		•^{2} $(\cos\theta + i\sin\theta)^4 = \cos^4\theta$ $+ 4\cos^3\theta(i\sin\theta) + 6\cos^2\theta(i\sin\theta)^2 + \ldots$
		•^{3} complete expansion		•^{3} $\cos^4\theta + 4\cos^3\theta(i\sin\theta) - 6\cos^2\theta\sin^2\theta$ $+ 4\cos\theta(i\sin\theta)^3 + \sin^4\theta$
		•^{4} identify and match real terms		•^{4} $\cos 4\theta = \cos^4\theta - 6\cos^2\theta\sin^2\theta + \sin^4\theta$
		•^{5} identify and match imaginary terms		•^{5} $\sin 4\theta = 4\cos^3\theta\sin\theta - 4\cos\theta\sin^3\theta$
	(b)	Ans: proof	3	
		•^{6} strategy		•^{6} $\tan 4\theta = \dfrac{\sin 4\theta}{\cos 4\theta}$ $= \dfrac{4\cos^3\theta\sin\theta - 4\cos\theta\sin^3\theta}{\cos^4\theta - 6\cos^2\theta\sin^2\theta + \sin^4\theta}$
		•^{7} divide numerator and denominator by $\cos^4 x$		•^{7} $\dfrac{\dfrac{4\cos^3\theta\sin\theta}{\cos^4\theta} - \dfrac{4\cos\theta\sin^3\theta}{\cos^4\theta}}{\dfrac{\cos^4\theta}{\cos^4\theta} - \dfrac{6\cos^2\theta\sin^2\theta}{\cos^4\theta} + \dfrac{\sin^4\theta}{\cos^4\theta}}$
		•^{8} complete		•^{8} $\dfrac{\dfrac{4\sin\theta}{\cos\theta} - \dfrac{4\sin^3\theta}{\cos^3\theta}}{1 - \dfrac{6\sin^2\theta}{\cos^2\theta} + \dfrac{\sin^4\theta}{\cos^4\theta}} = \dfrac{4\tan\theta - 4\tan^3\theta}{1 - 6\tan^2\theta + \tan^4\theta}$

Question		Expected response (Give one mark for each •)	Max mark	Additional guidance (Illustration of evidence for awarding a mark at each •)
	(c)	Ans: $\theta = \dfrac{\pi}{16}$ and $\dfrac{5\pi}{16}$ •⁹ strategy •¹⁰ complete process and find a solution for 4θ •¹¹ find both solutions	3	•⁹ $\tan^4\theta + 4\tan^3\theta - 6\tan^2\theta - 4\tan\theta + 1 = 0$ $4\tan\theta - 4\tan^3\theta = 1 - 6\tan^2\theta + \tan^4\theta$ $\dfrac{4\tan\theta - 4\tan^3\theta}{1 - 6\tan^2\theta + \tan^4\theta} = 1$ •¹⁰ $\tan 4\theta = 1,\ 4\theta = \dfrac{\pi}{4}$ •¹¹ $\theta = \dfrac{\pi}{16}$ and $\dfrac{5\pi}{16}$

ADVANCED HIGHER MATHEMATICS
MODEL PAPER

Question	Expected response (Give one mark for each •)	Additional guidance (Illustration of evidence for awarding a mark at each •)	Max mark
1. (a)	Ans: $x = 2$ and $x = -\dfrac{1}{4}$ •^{1} correct use of product rule •^{2} factorise $f'(x)$ •^{3} solve $f'(x) = 0$	•^{1} $f'(x) = (x-2)^3 + 3(x+1)(x-2)^2$ •^{2} $f'(x) = (x-2)^2(4x+1)$ •^{3} $x = 2$ and $x = -\dfrac{1}{4}$	3
(b)	Ans: $-\dfrac{1}{2}$ **Method 1** •^{4} differentiate LHS of equation •^{5} differentiate RHS of equation •^{6} substitute for x and y or find $\dfrac{dy}{dx}$ •^{7} find gradient of curve **Method 2** •^{4} start to differentiate using quotient rule •^{5} complete differentiation •^{6} substitute for x and y **or** find $\dfrac{dy}{dx}$ •^{7} find gradient of curve	•^{4} $2x + x\dfrac{dy}{dx} + y = \ldots$ •^{5} $2x + x\dfrac{dy}{dx} + y = 2y\dfrac{dy}{dx} - 5\dfrac{dy}{dx}$ •^{6} $6 + 3\dfrac{dy}{dx} - 1 = -2\dfrac{dy}{dx} - 5\dfrac{dy}{dx}$ **or** $\dfrac{dy}{dx} = \dfrac{2x+y}{2y-x-5}$ •^{7} $5 = -10\dfrac{dy}{dx} \Rightarrow \dfrac{dy}{dx} = -\dfrac{1}{2}$ **or** $\dfrac{dy}{dx} = \dfrac{6-1}{-2-3-5} = \dfrac{5}{-10} = -\dfrac{1}{2}$ •^{4} $\dfrac{2xy - \ldots}{y^2}$ •^{5} $\dfrac{2xy - x^2\dfrac{dy}{dx}}{y^2} + 1 = \dfrac{dy}{dx}$ •^{6} $\dfrac{-6 - 9\dfrac{dy}{dx}}{1} + 1 = \dfrac{dy}{dx}$ **or** $\dfrac{dy}{dx} = \dfrac{2xy + y^2}{x^2 + y^2}$ •^{7} $-5 = 10\dfrac{dy}{dx} \Rightarrow \dfrac{dy}{dx} = -\dfrac{1}{2}$ **or** $\dfrac{dy}{dx} = \dfrac{-6+1}{9+1} = \dfrac{-5}{10} = -\dfrac{1}{2}$	4

Question			Expected response (Give one mark for each •)	Additional guidance (Illustration of evidence for awarding a mark at each •)	Max mark
2.			Ans: 6225		4
			•¹ use $u_n = a + (n-1)d$	•¹ $u_{20} = 97 \Rightarrow a + 19d = 97$	
			•² find d	•² $a = 2 \Rightarrow 2 + 19d = 97 \Rightarrow d = 5$	
			•³ know to use formula for S_n	•³ $S_n = \dfrac{n}{2}[2a + (n-1)d]$	
			•⁴ find S_{50}	•⁴ $\dfrac{50}{2}[4 + 49 \times 5] = 6225$	
3.			Ans: $3 - 3i$ and -6		4
			•¹ show that $3 + 3i$ is a root of the equation	•¹ $(3+3i)^3 = 27 + 81i + 81i^2 + 27i^3 = -54 + 54i$ $\Rightarrow (3+3i)^3 - 18(3+3i) + 108$ $= -54 + 54i - 54 - 54i + 108$ $= 0$	
			•² find conjugate root	•² $3 - 3i$	
			•³ find quadratic factor	•³ $(z-(3+3i))(z-(3-3i)) = z^2 - 6z + 18$	
			•⁴ find remaining root	•⁴ $z^3 - 18z + 108 = (z^2 - 6z + 18)(z + 6)$ so remaining roots are $3 - 3i$ and -6	
4.	(a)		Ans: $x = \pm 2$		2
			•¹ find determinant of matrix A	•¹ $\det A = 4 - x^2$	
			•² solve $\det A = 0$	•² $4 - x^2 = 0 \Rightarrow x = \pm 2$	
	(b)		Ans: $q = 125$		3
			•³ show that $A^2 = 5A$	•³ $A^2 = \begin{pmatrix} 1 & 2 \\ 2 & 4 \end{pmatrix}\begin{pmatrix} 1 & 2 \\ 2 & 4 \end{pmatrix} = \begin{pmatrix} 5 & 10 \\ 10 & 20 \end{pmatrix} = 5A$	
			•⁴ begin to express A^4 in terms of A	•⁴ $A^4 = (A^2)^2 = (5A)^2 = \dots$	
			•⁵ show that $A^4 = 125A$	•⁵ $\dots (5A)^2 = 25A^2 = 125A \Rightarrow q = 125$	
5.	(a)		Ans: $1 + 5x + 10x^2 + 10x^3 + 5x^4 + x^5$		1
			•¹ expand $(1 + x)^5$	•¹ $1 + 5x + 10x^2 + 10x^3 + 5x^4 + x^5$	
	(b)		Ans: proof		2
			•² substitute $x = -0.1$ into $(1 + x)^5$	•² $0.9^5 = (1 + (-0.1))^5$	
			•³ expand $(1 + (-0.1))^5$ and show steps leading to 0.59049	•³ $1 - 0.5 + 0.1 - 0.01 + 0.0005 - 0.00001$ $= 0.59049$	

Question			Expected response (Give one mark for each •)	Additional guidance (Illustration of evidence for awarding a mark at each •)	Max mark
6.			Ans: $\dfrac{3}{8}$		5
			•^{1} differentiate $x = 1 + \sin\theta$	•^{1} $x = 1 + \sin\theta \;\Rightarrow\; dx = \cos\theta\, d\theta$	
			•^{2} find limits in terms of x	•^{2} $\theta = 0 \;\Rightarrow\; x = 1$ $\theta = \dfrac{\pi}{2} \;\Rightarrow\; x = 2$	
			•^{3} state integral in terms of x	•^{3} $\displaystyle\int_1^2 \frac{1}{x^3}\, dx$	
			•^{4} integrate correctly	•^{4} $\left[\dfrac{x^{-2}}{-2} \right]_1^2$	
			•^{5} evaluate integral	•^{5} $\dfrac{3}{8}$	
7.			Ans: $f(x) = 1 + x^2 - \dfrac{x^4}{3}$		4
			•^{1} evaluate $f(0)$	•^{1} $f(0) = 1$	
			•^{2} evaluate $f'(0)$ and $f''(0)$	•^{2} $f'(x) = 2\sin x \cos x = \sin 2x \;\Rightarrow\; f'(0) = 0$ $f''(x) = 2\cos 2x \;\Rightarrow\; f''(0) = 2$	
			•^{3} evaluate $f'''(0)$ and $f''''(0)$	•^{3} $f'''(x) = -4\sin 2x \;\Rightarrow\; f'''(0) = 0$ $f''''(x) = -8\cos 2x \;\Rightarrow\; f''''(0) = -8$	
			•^{4} state first three terms of $f(x)$	•^{4} $f(x) = 1 + x^2 - \dfrac{x^4}{3}$	
8.			Ans: proof		5
			•^{1} show true when $n = 1$	•^{1} When $n = 1$, LHS $= \dfrac{1}{1 \times 2} = \dfrac{1}{2}$, RHS $= 1 - \dfrac{1}{2} = \dfrac{1}{2}$. So true when $n = 1$.	
			•^{2} assume true for $n = k$	•^{2} Assume true for $n = k$, $\displaystyle\sum_{r=1}^{k} \frac{1}{r(r+1)} = 1 - \frac{1}{k+1}$	
			•^{3} consider $n = k+1$	•^{3} Consider $n = k+1$, $\displaystyle\sum_{r=1}^{k+1} \frac{1}{r(r+1)} = \sum_{r=1}^{k} \frac{1}{r(r+1)} + \frac{1}{(k+1)(k+2)}$	
			•^{4} simplify	•^{4} $= 1 - \dfrac{1}{k+1} + \dfrac{1}{(k+1)(k+2)}$ $= 1 - \dfrac{k+2-1}{(k+1)(k+2)}$ $= 1 - \dfrac{k+1}{(k+1)((k+1)+1)}$	
			•^{5} express in required form and state conclusion	•^{5} $= 1 - \dfrac{1}{((k+1)+1)}$ Thus, if true for $n = k$, statement is true for $n = k+1$, and, since true for $n = 1$, true for all $n \geq 1$.	

Question			Expected response (Give one mark for each •)	Additional guidance (Illustration of evidence for awarding a mark at each •)	Max mark
9.			Ans: $y = A\exp\left(2(1+x)^{\frac{3}{2}}\right) - 1$		5
			Method 1		
			•^{1} separate the variables	•^{1} $\int \dfrac{dy}{1+y} = 3\int (1+x)^{\frac{1}{2}}\,dx$	
			•^{2} integrate term in y	•^{2} $\ln(1+y) = \ldots$	
			•^{3} integrate term in x	•^{3} $\ln(1+y) = 2(1+x)^{\frac{3}{2}} + \ldots$	
			•^{4} insert constant and eliminate ln	•^{4} $1+y = \exp\left(2(1+x)^{\frac{3}{2}} + c\right)$	
			•^{5} solve for y	•^{5} $y = \exp\left(2(1+x)^{\frac{3}{2}} + c\right) - 1$ $= A\exp\left(2(1+x)^{\frac{3}{2}}\right) - 1$	
			Method 2		
			•^{1} express in form $\dfrac{dy}{dx} + P(x)y = Q(x)$	•^{1} $\dfrac{dy}{dx} - 3\left(\sqrt{1+x}\right)y = 3\sqrt{1+x}$	
			•^{2} find integrating factor	•^{2} $\exp\left(-3\int \sqrt{1+x}\,dx\right) = \exp\left(-2(1+x)^{\frac{3}{2}}\right)$	
			•^{3} express as derivative of product	•^{3} $\dfrac{d}{dx}y\exp\left(-2(1+x)^{\frac{3}{2}}\right)$ $= 3\sqrt{1+x}\exp\left(-2(1+x)^{\frac{3}{2}}\right)$	
			•^{4} integrate	•^{4} $y\exp\left(-2(1+x)^{\frac{3}{2}}\right)$ $= -\int\left(-3\sqrt{1+x}\right)\exp\left(-2(1+x)^{\frac{3}{2}}\right)dx$ $= -\exp\left(-2(1+x)^{\frac{3}{2}}\right) + c$	
			•^{5} solve for y	•^{5} $y = -1 + c\exp\left(2(1+x)^{\frac{3}{2}}\right)$	

Question			Expected response (Give one mark for each •)	Additional guidance (Illustration of evidence for awarding a mark at each •)	Max mark
10.			Ans: $\dfrac{\pi}{8} - \dfrac{1}{4}\ln 2$		5
			•¹ start to integrate by parts	•¹ $\left[\tan^{-1}x^2 \int x\,dx\right]_0^1 \cdots$	
			•² continue to integrate by parts	•² $\cdots - \displaystyle\int_0^1 \dfrac{x^3}{1+x^4}\,dx$	
			•³ integrate correctly	•³ $\left[\dfrac{1}{2}x^2\tan^{-1}x^2\right]_0^1 - \left[\dfrac{1}{4}\ln(1+x^4)\right]_0^1$	
			•⁴ substitute limits	•⁴ $\dfrac{1}{2}\tan^{-1}1 - 0 - \left(\dfrac{1}{4}\ln 2 - \dfrac{1}{4}\ln 1\right)$	
			•⁵ evaluate integral	•⁵ $\dfrac{\pi}{8} - \dfrac{1}{4}\ln 2$	
11.	(a)		Ans: 32		1
			•¹ find acceleration when $t = 0$	•¹ $a = \dfrac{dv}{dt} = 3t^2 - 24t + 32$ $\Rightarrow$ when $t = 0$, $a = 32$	
	(b)		Ans: $s = \dfrac{1}{4}t^4 - 4t^3 + 16t^2$; $t = 8$		4
			•² integrate to find general formula for displacement	•² $s = \displaystyle\int t^3 - 12t^2 + 32t\,dt = \dfrac{1}{4}t^4 - 4t^3 + 16t^2 + c$	
			•³ find formula for displacement when $t = 0$	•³ $s = 0$ when $t = 0 \Rightarrow c = 0$ $\Rightarrow s = \dfrac{1}{4}t^4 - 4t^3 + 16t^2$	
			•⁴ set displacement equal to 0 and factorise	•⁴ at O, $s = 0 \Rightarrow \dfrac{1}{4}t^4 - 4t^3 + 16t^2 = 0$ $\Leftrightarrow \dfrac{1}{4}t^2(t^2 - 16t + 64) = 0$ $\Leftrightarrow \dfrac{1}{4}t^2(t-8)^2 = 0$	
			•⁵ state time that body returns to O	•⁵ the body returns to O when $t = 8$	

Question	Expected response (Give one mark for each •)	Additional guidance (Illustration of evidence for awarding a mark at each •)	Max mark
12.	Ans: $a = 4$, $b = 2$, $c = -3$; diagram		4
	•1 substitute $z = x + iy$ into given equation	•1 $\|z - 2\| = \|z + i\|$ $\Leftrightarrow \|(x - 2) + iy\| = \|x + (y + 1)i\|$	
	•2 find expressions for the square of each modulus	•2 $(x - 2)^2 + y^2 = x^2 + (y + 1)^2$	
	•3 rearrange into the form $ax + by + c = 0$	•3 $x^2 - 4x + 4 + y^2 = x^2 + y^2 + 2y + 1$ $\Leftrightarrow 4x + 2y - 3 = 0$	
	•4 show locus on Argand diagram	•4	
13.	Ans: proof		4
	•1 state assumption that $2 + x$ is rational	•1 Assume $2 + x$ is rational	
	•2 express $2 + x$ as a rational number	•2 and let $2 + x = \dfrac{p}{q}$ where p, q are integers.	
	•3 rearrange to express x as a rational number	•3 So $x = \dfrac{p}{q} - 2 = \dfrac{p - 2q}{q}$.	
	•4 state conclusion	•4 Since $p - 2q$ and q are integers, it follows that x is rational. This is a contradiction.	

Question			Expected response (Give one mark for each •)	Additional guidance (Illustration of evidence for awarding a mark at each •)	Max mark
14.			Ans: $$y = -4e^x + e^{2x} + x^2 + 3x + \frac{7}{2}$$		10
			•^{1} state the auxiliary equation	•^{1} $m^2 - 3m + 2 = 0$	
			•^{2} solve the auxiliary equation	•^{2} $(m-1)(m-2) = 0 \implies m = 1$ or $m = 2$	
			•^{3} state the complementary function	•^{3} $y = Ae^x + Be^{2x}$	
			•^{4} use correct form of particular integral	•^{4} $y = ax^2 + bx + c$	
			•^{5} substitute for $\frac{d^2y}{dx^2}, \frac{dy}{dx}$ and y in the differential equation	•^{5} $\frac{dy}{dx} = 2ax + b, \frac{d^2y}{dx^2} = 2a$ $\implies 2a - 3(2ax + b) + 2(ax^2 + bx + c) = 2x^2$	
			•^{6} find values of a, b and c	•^{6} $\Leftrightarrow 2ax^2 + (-6a + 2b)x + (2a - 3b + 2c) = 2x^2$ $\implies a = 1, b = 3, c = \frac{7}{2}$	
			•^{7} state general solution	•^{7} $y = Ae^x + Be^{2x} + x^2 + 3x + \frac{7}{2}$	
			•^{8} obtain equation in A and B by substituting $x = 0$, $y = \frac{1}{2}$ and $\frac{dy}{dx} = 1$ into the general solution	•^{8} $\frac{1}{2} = A + B + \frac{7}{2} \implies A + B = -3$	
			•^{9} obtain equation in A and B by substituting $x = 0$, $y = \frac{1}{2}$ and $\frac{dy}{dx} = 1$ into the derivative of the general solution	•^{9} $\frac{dy}{dx} = Ae^x + 2Be^{2x} + 2x + 3$ $\implies 1 = A + 2B + 3$ $\implies A + 2B = -2$	
			•^{10} state particular solution	•^{10} $A = -4, B = 1$ $\implies y = -4e^x + e^{2x} + x^2 + 3x + \frac{7}{2}$	

Question	Expected response (Give one mark for each •)	Additional guidance (Illustration of evidence for awarding a mark at each •)	Max mark
15.	Ans: $\sqrt{2}$		10
	•¹ correct form of partial fractions	•¹ $\dfrac{A}{x}+\dfrac{Bx+C}{x^2+1}$	
	•² find value of A	•² $1=A(x^2+1)+(Bx+C)x$ $x=0 \;\Rightarrow\; A=1$	
	•³ set up equations in B and C	•³ $x=1 \;\Rightarrow\; 1=2+B+C$ $x=-1 \;\Rightarrow\; 1=2+B-C$	
	•⁴ express integral in partial fractions	•⁴ $B=-1,\; C=0$ $\Rightarrow\; I(k)=\displaystyle\int_{1}^{k}\left(\dfrac{1}{x}-\dfrac{x}{x^2+1}\right)dx$	
	•⁵ integrate first fraction	•⁵ $\displaystyle\int_{1}^{k}\dfrac{1}{x}\,dx=\left[\ln x\right]_{1}^{k}$	
	•⁶ integrate second fraction	•⁶ $\dfrac{1}{2}\displaystyle\int_{1}^{k}\dfrac{2x}{x^2+1}=\dfrac{1}{2}\left[\ln(x^2+1)\right]_{1}^{k}$	
	•⁷ substitute limits	•⁷ $\ln k-\ln 1-\dfrac{1}{2}\ln(k^2+1)+\dfrac{1}{2}\ln 2$	
	•⁸ express integral in required form	•⁸ $\ln\dfrac{k\sqrt{2}}{\sqrt{k^2+1}}$	
	•⁹ state expression for $e^{I(k)}$	•⁹ $\dfrac{k\sqrt{2}}{\sqrt{k^2+1}}$	
	•¹⁰ evaluate $\lim\limits_{k\to\infty} e^{I(k)}$	•¹⁰ $\dfrac{\sqrt{2}}{\sqrt{1+k^{-2}}}\to\sqrt{2}$ as $k\to\infty$	
16. (a)	Ans: $f'(x)=\dfrac{\ln x-1}{(\ln x)^2}$ $f''(x)=\dfrac{2-\ln x}{x(\ln x)^3}$		4
	•¹ start to use quotient rule to find $f'(x)$	•¹ $\dfrac{1\times\ln x-\ldots}{(\ln x)^2}$	
	•² find $f'(x)$ in simplest form	•² $\dfrac{1\times\ln x-x\times\dfrac{1}{x}}{(\ln x)^2}=\dfrac{\ln x-1}{(\ln x)^2}$	
	•³ use quotient rule to find $f''(x)$	•³ $\dfrac{\dfrac{1}{x}\times(\ln x)^2-(\ln x-1)\times\dfrac{2\ln x}{x}}{(\ln x)^4}$	
	•⁴ find $f''(x)$ in simplest form	•⁴ $\dfrac{\ln x-2\ln x+2}{x(\ln x)^3}=\dfrac{2-\ln x}{x(\ln x)^3}$	

Question	Expected response (Give one mark for each •)	Additional guidance (Illustration of evidence for awarding a mark at each •)	Max mark
(b)	Ans: (e, e); minimum turning point. •[5] find coordinates of stationary point •[6] find sign of f'' at stationary point •[7] state nature of stationary point	•[5] $f'(x) = 0$ when $\ln x = 1$ $\Rightarrow x = e$ and $y = e$ •[6] At (e, e), $f''(e) = \dfrac{2-1}{e \times 1^3} > 0$ •[7] Hence (e, e) is a minimum turning point.	3
(c)	Ans: $\left(e^2, \dfrac{1}{2}e^2\right)$ •[8] find x coordinate of the point of inflexion •[9] state the coordinates of the point of inflexion	•[8] $f''(x) = 0$ when $\ln x = 2 \Rightarrow x = e^2$ •[9] $x = e^2 \Rightarrow y = \dfrac{1}{2}e^2$, so the point of inflexion is $\left(e^2, \dfrac{1}{2}e^2\right)$	2
17. (a)	Ans: $x = 3$, $y = -2$, $z = -5$ •[1] set up augmented matrix •[2] eliminate the x terms from rows 2 and 3 •[3] eliminate the y term from row 3 •[4] solve for z •[5] solve for x and y	•[1] $\left[\begin{array}{ccc\|c} 1 & 1 & -1 & 6 \\ 2 & -3 & 2 & 2 \\ -5 & 2 & \lambda & 1 \end{array}\right]$ •[2] $\Rightarrow \left[\begin{array}{ccc\|c} 1 & 1 & -1 & 6 \\ 0 & -5 & 4 & -10 \\ 0 & 7 & \lambda-5 & 31 \end{array}\right]$ •[3] $\Rightarrow \left[\begin{array}{ccc\|c} 1 & 1 & -1 & 6 \\ 0 & -5 & 4 & -10 \\ 0 & 0 & 5\lambda+3 & 85 \end{array}\right]$ •[4] $z = \dfrac{85}{5\lambda+3}$ •[5] $z = -5$ $-5y - 20 = -10 \Rightarrow y = -2$ $x - 2 + 5 = 6 \Rightarrow x = 3$	5

Question			Expected response (Give one mark for each •)	Additional guidance (Illustration of evidence for awarding a mark at each •)	Max mark
	(b)		Ans: proof		2
			•^{6} eliminate y and z in system of equations	•^{6} $\begin{aligned} x + y - z &= 6 \quad &(1)\\ 2x - 3y + 2z &= 2 \quad &(2)\\ 5x \quad\;\; - z &= 20 \quad &(2) + 3\,(1)\\ 4x - y \quad\;\; &= 14 \quad &(2) + 2\,(1) \end{aligned}$	
			•^{7} use equations to show that $y = 4t - 14$ and $z = 5t - 20$ given that $x = t$	•^{7} $y = 4x - 14$ $z = 5x - 20$ $x = t,\; y = 4t - 14,\; z = 5t - 20$	
	(c)		Ans: 23·0°		4
			•^{8} know how to find angle between the line and the plane	•^{8} evidence of $\cos\theta = \dfrac{l \cdot n}{|l||n|}$ where $\theta =$ the angle between the line and the plane, $l =$ the direction of the line and $n =$ the direction of the normal to the plane	
			•^{9} find $l \cdot n$, $\lvert l \rvert$ and $\lvert n \rvert$	•^{9} $l = i + 4j + 5k$ and $n = -5i + 2j - 4k$ $\Rightarrow \cos\theta = \dfrac{l \cdot n}{\lvert l \rvert\lvert n \rvert} = \dfrac{-17}{\sqrt{42}\sqrt{45}}$	
			•^{10} find angle between the line and the normal to the plane	•^{10} 113·0°	
			•^{11} find acute angle between the line and the plane	•^{11} 113·0° − 90° = 23·0°	

ADVANCED HIGHER MATHEMATICS 2016

Question		Generic scheme	Illustrative scheme	Max mark
1.	(a)	$\bullet^1$ evidence of use of product rule[1,2]	$\bullet^1$ $(...)\tan^{-1}2x + x(...)$	3
		$\bullet^2$ one resultant term of the product correct	$\bullet^2$ $1.\tan^{-1}2x$ or $x.\dfrac{1}{1+(2x)^2}.2$	
		$\bullet^3$ complete differentiation[3]	$\bullet^3$ $\tan^{-1}2x + \dfrac{2x}{1+4x^2}$	

Notes:

1. Evidence for the award of $\bullet^1$ should take the form $f(x)\times(...) + g(x)\times(...)$.

2. For a candidate who interprets $\tan^{-1}2x$ as $(\tan 2x)^{-1}$ $\bullet^3$ is not available.

3. Accept $(2x)^2$ when awarding $\bullet^3$.

	(b)	$\bullet^4$ evidence of use of quotient or product rule and one term of numerator correct	$\bullet^4$ $(-2x)(1+4x^2)-$	3
		$\bullet^5$ complete differentiation correctly	$\bullet^5$ $\dfrac{...(1-x^2).8x}{(1+4x^2)^2}$	
		$\bullet^6$ simplify answer[4,5]	$\bullet^6$ $-\dfrac{10x}{(1+4x^2)^2}$ or $\dfrac{-10x}{(1+4x^2)^2}$	

Notes:

4. Where a candidate uses the product rule, simplification to $-\dfrac{10x}{(1+4x^2)^2}$ or $-10x(1+4x^2)^{-2}$ will be required in order to obtain $\bullet^6$.

5. Incorrect working subsequent to a correct answer should be penalised in this instance eg an incorrect expansion of the denominator

	(c)	$\bullet^7$ correct derivatives	$\bullet^7$ 6 and $\sin t$	2
		$\bullet^8$ find $\dfrac{dy}{dx}$	$\bullet^8$ $\dfrac{1}{6}\sin t$	

Question		Generic scheme	Illustrative scheme	Max mark
2.	(a)	$\bullet^1$ interpret geometric series $\bullet^2$ evidence of strategy[1,2] $\bullet^3$ value[2]	$\bullet^1$ $ar = 108$ and $ar^4 = 4$ $\bullet^2$ $\dfrac{ar^4}{ar}$ $r^3 = \dfrac{1}{27}$ $\bullet^3$ $r = \dfrac{1}{3}$	3

Notes:
1. For $\bullet^2$ accept $r^3 = \dfrac{1}{27}$.
2. For a statement of the answer only, award $\bullet^1$ and $\bullet^3$. To earn $\bullet^2$ there must be evidence of a strategy eg $108 \to 36 \to 12 \to 4$ gives $r = \dfrac{1}{3}$.

| | (b) | $\bullet^4$ know condition[3,4] | $\bullet^4$ $-1 < \dfrac{1}{3} < 1$ | 1 |

Notes:
3. For $\bullet^4$ $\frac{1}{3}$ may be replaced with a letter consistent with their answer to (a). However, in the case where a candidate obtains a value in (a) outside the open interval $(-1, 1)$ $\bullet^4$ will only be available where they also acknowledge that there is no sum to infinity.
4. Only award $\bullet^4$ for a strict inequality, whether it is expressed algebraically or in words.

| | (c) | $\bullet^5$ calculate the first term

$\bullet^6$ value[5,6] | $\bullet^5$ $a = 324$

$\bullet^6$ $\dfrac{324}{1 - \dfrac{1}{3}}$ or equivalent leading to 486 | 2 |

Notes:
5. For an incorrect value in (a) $\bullet^6$ will only be available provided the value satisfies the condition for convergence.
6. Where a candidate has used $S_\infty = \dfrac{a\left(1 - r^\infty\right)}{1 - r}$ full credit is available.

Question			Generic scheme	Illustrative scheme	Max mark
3.		$\bullet^1$	state general term[2]	$\bullet^1$ $\ {}^{13}C_r\left(\dfrac{3}{x}\right)^{13-r}(-2x)^r$	5
		$\bullet^2$	simplify powers of x OR coefficients **and** signs[2,5]	$\bullet^2$ $\ (3)^{13-r}(-2)^r$ or x^{2r-13}	
		$\bullet^3$	state simplified general term (completes simplification)[2,5]	$\bullet^3$ $\ {}^{13}C_r(3)^{13-r}(-2)^r x^{2r-13}$	
		$\bullet^4$	determine value of r[3,4]	$\bullet^4$ $\ 2r-13=9 \Rightarrow r=11$	
		$\bullet^5$	evaluate term[1,3]	$\bullet^5$ $\ -1437696x^9$	

Notes:
1. Accept -1437696.
2. For $\bullet^1$ accept the initial appearance of $\displaystyle\sum_{r=0}^{13} {}^{13}C_r\left(\dfrac{3}{x}\right)^{13-r}(-2x)^r$ as bad form. $\bullet^2$ and $\bullet^3$ are

   available only to candidates who simplify a general term correctly.
3. $\bullet^4$ and $\bullet^5$ are the only marks available to candidates who have not proceeded from a general term eg. an expansion using Pascal's Triangle. The required term must be explicitly identified in order for $\bullet^5$ to be awarded.
4. Starting with ${}^{13}C_r\left(\dfrac{3}{x}\right)^r(-2x)^{13-r}$ leading to $r=2$ can also gain full credit.

5. Accept $\dfrac{1}{x^{13-2r}}$ when awarding $\bullet^2$ or $\bullet^3$.

Question			Generic scheme	Illustrative scheme	Max mark
4.		$\bullet^1$	Construct augmented matrix	$\bullet^1$ $\begin{pmatrix} 1 & 2 & 3 & \vdots & 3 \\ 2 & -1 & 4 & \vdots & 5 \\ 1 & -3 & 2\lambda & \vdots & 2 \end{pmatrix}$	4
		$\bullet^2$	Use row operations to establish first two zero elements[1]	$\bullet^2$ $\begin{pmatrix} 1 & 2 & 3 & \vdots & 3 \\ 0 & 5 & 2 & \vdots & 1 \\ 0 & -5 & 2\lambda-3 & \vdots & -1 \end{pmatrix}$	
		$\bullet^3$	Establish third zero element **OR** recognise linear relationship between two rows[1,2]	$\bullet^3$ $\begin{pmatrix} 1 & 2 & 3 & \vdots & 3 \\ 0 & 5 & 2 & \vdots & 1 \\ 0 & 0 & 2\lambda-1 & \vdots & 0 \end{pmatrix}$ **or** $2\lambda-3=-2$	
		$\bullet^4$	State value of λ[2]	$\bullet^4$ $\ \lambda=\dfrac{1}{2}$	

Notes:
1. Elementary row operations must be carried out correctly for $\bullet^2$ and $\bullet^3$ to be awarded.
2. $\bullet^4$ is only available where a candidate's final matrix exhibits redundancy.
3. Disregard any working/statement subsequent to $\lambda=\dfrac{1}{2}$.

Question	Generic scheme	Illustrative scheme	Max mark
5.	**PROOF** •^{1} show true for $n=1$[1] •^{2} assume true for $n=k$[2] **and** consider $n=k+1$ •^{3} correct statement of sum to $(k+1)$ terms using inductive hypothesis •^{4} express explicitly in terms of $(k+1)$ **or** achieve stated aim/goal[3,4] **and** communicate	**PROOF** •^{1} LHS: $1(3-1)=2$ RHS: $1^2(1+1)=2$ So true for $n=1$ •^{2} $\displaystyle\sum_{r=1}^{k} r(3r-1)=k^2(k+1)$ **and** $\displaystyle\sum_{r=1}^{k+1} r(3r-1)=$ $\displaystyle\ldots=\sum_{r=1}^{k} r(3r-1)+(k+1)(3(k+1)-1)$ •^{3} $=k^2(k+1)+(k+1)(3k+2)$ $=(k+1)\left[k^2+3k+2\right]$ $=(k+1)(k+1)(k+2)$ •^{4} $=(k+1)^2\big((k+1)+1\big)$, thus if true for $n=k$ then true for $n=k+1$ but since true for $n=1$, then by induction true for all $n\in\mathbb{N}$	4

Notes:

1. "RHS = 2, LHS = 2" and/or "True for $n=1$" are insufficient for the award of •^{1}. A candidate must demonstrate evidence of substitution into both expressions.

2. For •^{2} acceptable phrases include: "If true for…"; "Suppose true for…"; "Assume true for…". However, *not* acceptable: "Consider $n=k$", "assume $n=k$" and "True for $n=k$". **Allow if appears at conclusion.**

3. Full marks are available to candidates who state an aim/goal earlier in the proof and who subsequently achieve the stated aim/goal.

4. Minimum acceptable form for •^{4}: "Then true for $n=k+1$, but since true for $n=1$, then true for all n" or equivalent.

Question	Generic scheme	Illustrative scheme	Max mark
6.	**Method 1** $\bullet^1$ for either function: first derivative and two evaluations **OR** all three derivatives **OR** all four evaluations	$\bullet^1$ $f(x)=\sin 3x \qquad f(0)=0$ $f'(x)=3\cos 3x \qquad f'(0)=3$ $f''(x)=-9\sin 3x \qquad f''(0)=0$ $f'''(x)=-27\cos 3x \qquad f'''(0)=-27$ $f(x)=f(0)+f'(0)x+\dfrac{f''(0)}{2!}x^2+\dfrac{f'''(0)}{3!}x^3\ldots$	6
	$\bullet^2$ complete derivatives and evaluations **AND** substitute	$\bullet^2$ $f(x)=3x-\dfrac{27}{3!}x^3$ $=3x-\dfrac{9}{2}x^3$	
	$\bullet^3$ for second function: first derivative and two evaluations **OR** all three derivatives **OR** all four evaluations	$\bullet^3$ $f(x)=e^{4x} \qquad f(0)=1$ $f'(x)=4e^{4x} \qquad f'(0)=4$ $f''(x)=16e^{4x} \quad f''(0)=16$ $f'''(x)=64e^{4x} \quad f'''(0)=64$	
	$\bullet^4$ complete derivatives and evaluations **AND** substitute	$\bullet^4$ $f(x)=1+4x+\dfrac{16x^2}{2}+\dfrac{64x^3}{6}$ $=1+4x+8x^2+\dfrac{32}{3}x^3$	
	$\bullet^5$ multiply expressions	$\bullet^5$ $e^{4x}\sin 3x=\left(3x-\dfrac{9}{2}x^3\ldots\right)\left(1+4x+8x^2+\dfrac{32}{3}x^3\ldots\right)$ $=24x^3-\dfrac{9}{2}x^3+12x^2+3x\ldots$	
	$\bullet^6$ multiply out and simplify[Note 2]	$\bullet^6$ $=3x+12x^2+\dfrac{39}{2}x^3\ldots$	

Notes:

1. If a candidate chooses to use the product rule to obtain the Maclaurin series for $e^{4x}\sin 3x$ without first obtaining series for e^{4x} and $\sin 3x$ separately then only $\bullet^5$ and $\bullet^6$ are potentially available. In this instance for the award of $\bullet^5$ apply the same principle as that used to award $\bullet^1$ and $\bullet^3$.

$f(x)=e^{4x}\sin 3x \qquad\qquad f(0)=0$

$f'(x)=4e^{4x}\sin 3x+3e^{4x}\cos 3x \qquad f'(0)=3$

$f''(x)=7e^{4x}\sin 3x+24e^{4x}\cos 3x \qquad f''(0)=24$

$f'''(x)=-44e^{4x}\sin 3x+117e^{4x}\cos 3x \qquad f'''(0)=117$

2. At $\bullet^6$ the appearance of terms in x^4 or above should be disregarded.

Question	Generic scheme	Illustrative scheme	Max mark
	Method 2		
	•^{1} state the Maclaurin expansion for $\sin x$ [1]	•^{1} $\sin x = x - \dfrac{x^3}{3!}...$	
	•^{2} substitute	•^{2} $\sin 3x = 3x - \dfrac{(3x)^3}{3!}...$ $\sin 3x = 3x - \dfrac{9x^3}{2}...$	
	•^{3} state the Maclaurin expansion for e^x [1]	•^{3} $e^x = 1 + x + \dfrac{x^2}{2!} + \dfrac{x^3}{3!}...$	
	•^{4} substitute	•^{4} $e^{4x} = 1 + 4x + \dfrac{(4x)^2}{2!} + \dfrac{(4x)^3}{3!}...$ $e^{4x} = 1 + 4x + 8x^2 + \dfrac{32x^3}{3}...$	
	•^{5} multiply expressions	•^{5} $e^{4x}\sin 3x = \left(1 + 4x + 8x^2...\right)\left(3x - \dfrac{9x^3}{2}...\right)$	
	•^{6} multiply out and simplify	•^{6} $e^{4x}\sin 3x = 3x + 12x^2 + \dfrac{39x^3}{2} + ...$	

Notes:
1. For a candidate who writes down $\sin 3x = 3x - \dfrac{(3x)^3}{3!}...$ without first writing down the series for $\sin x$ then •^{1} may be awarded. A similar principle may be applied to the awarding of •^{3} if required.
2. At •^{6} the appearance of terms in x^4 or above should be disregarded.

7.	(a)		•^{1} calculate determinant [1]	•^{1} -2	1

Notes:
1. If a candidate chooses to find A^{-1} then •^{1} is only available where '$\det A$' is clearly identified.

Question			Generic scheme	Illustrative scheme	Max mark
	(b)		**Method 1**		**3**
			•2 find A^2	•2 $A^2 = \begin{pmatrix} 4 & 0 \\ \lambda & 1 \end{pmatrix}$	
			•3 use an appropriate method	•3 $A^2 = \begin{pmatrix} 2 & 0 \\ \lambda & -1 \end{pmatrix} + \begin{pmatrix} 2 & 0 \\ 0 & 2 \end{pmatrix}$ $A^2 = A + 2I$	
			•4 write in required form and explicitly state values of p and q [Note 1]	•4 $p = 1$ **and** $q = 2$	
			Method 2		
			•2 find A^2	•2 $A^2 = \begin{pmatrix} 4 & 0 \\ \lambda & 1 \end{pmatrix}$	
			•3 use an appropriate method	•3 $A^2 = p\begin{pmatrix} 2 & 0 \\ \lambda & -1 \end{pmatrix} + q\begin{pmatrix} 1 & 0 \\ 0 & 1 \end{pmatrix}$	
			•4 write in required form and explicitly state values of p and q [Note 1]	•4 $A^2 = A + 2I$ $p = 1$ **and** $q = 2$	

Notes:

1. $\begin{pmatrix} 4 & 0 \\ \lambda & 1 \end{pmatrix} = \begin{pmatrix} 2 & 0 \\ \lambda & -1 \end{pmatrix} + 2\begin{pmatrix} 1 & 0 \\ 0 & 1 \end{pmatrix}$ is acceptable for •4 provided the values of p and q are explicitly stated.

Question			Generic scheme	Illustrative scheme	Max mark
	(c)		•5 square expression found in (b)[1,2,3]	•5 $A^4 = (A + 2I)^2$ $= A^2 + 4AI + 4I^2$ $= A + 2I + 4A + 4I$	**2**
			•6 substitute for A^2 and complete process	•6 $= 5A + 6I$	

Notes:
1. •5 may be obtained by squaring $\begin{pmatrix} 4 & 0 \\ \lambda & 1 \end{pmatrix}$ to give $\begin{pmatrix} 16 & 0 \\ 5\lambda & 1 \end{pmatrix}$ and identifying the coefficient of A as 5. This leads to •6 using the same method as in (b).
2. Accept equivalent expressions eg. $= A^2 + 4A + 4I$.
3. Candidates may calculate A^3 first so •5 can be awarded for $A^3 = 3A + 2I$.

Question	Generic scheme	Illustrative scheme	Max mark
8. (a)	•[1] correctly plot z on Argand diagram[1,2,3,4]	•[1]	1

Notes:
1. Do not penalise the omission of the diagonal line.
2. Treat alternative axis labels as bad form (to include the case where there are no labels).
3. Accept a point labelled using coordinates: $\left(\sqrt{3},-1\right)$ and, in this instance, $\left(\sqrt{3},-i\right)$.
4. The minimum acceptable response for the award of •[1] is a point in quadrant 4 together with $\sqrt{3}$ and -1 (or $-i$).

(b)	•[2] find modulus or argument[1,2,3,6]	•[2] $\left\|w\right\|=2a$ or $\arg(w)=-\dfrac{\pi}{6}$	2
	•[3] complete and express in polar form[3,4,5,6]	•[3] $w=2a\left(\cos\left(-\dfrac{\pi}{6}\right)+i\sin\left(-\dfrac{\pi}{6}\right)\right)$	

Notes:
1. For the award of •[2] and •[3] accept any answer of the form $-\dfrac{\pi}{6}+2k\pi,\ k\in\mathbb{Z}$.

2. For the award of •[2] and •[3] accept any answer of the form $\left(-30+360k\right)^\circ,\ k\in\mathbb{Z}$.
3. A candidate who chooses to work in degrees can only be awarded •[3] provided the degree symbol appears at some point within question 8.

4. Award •[3] for $w=2a\left(\cos\left(\dfrac{\pi}{6}\right)-i\sin\left(\dfrac{\pi}{6}\right)\right)$.

5. At •[3] do not accept $w=a\left[2\left(\cos\left(-\dfrac{\pi}{6}\right)+i\sin\left(-\dfrac{\pi}{6}\right)\right)\right]$.

6. Working subsequent to the appearance of $-\dfrac{\pi}{6}$ should be penalised where it leads to the use of an incorrect argument.

Question	Generic scheme	Illustrative scheme	Max mark
(c)	**Method 1**		3
	$\bullet^4$ process modulus	$\bullet^4$ $256a^8$	
	$\bullet^5$ process argument[1,2,3,4,5]	$\bullet^5$ $...\left(\cos\left(-\dfrac{8\pi}{6}\right)+i\sin\left(-\dfrac{8\pi}{6}\right)\right)$	
	$\bullet^6$ evaluate and express in form $ka^n\left(x+i\sqrt{y}\right)$	$\bullet^6$ $w^8=128a^8\left(-1+i\sqrt{3}\right)$	

Notes:

1. For the award of $\bullet^5$ accept any answer of the form $-\dfrac{4\pi}{3}+2k\pi,\ k\in\mathbb{Z}$.

2. For the award of $\bullet^5$ accept any answer of the form $\left(-240+360k\right)^\circ,\ k\in\mathbb{Z}$.
3. A candidate who chooses to work in degrees can only be awarded $\bullet^5$ provided the degree symbol appears at some point within question 8.
4. Do not penalise unsimplified fractions.

5. Award $\bullet^5$ for $...\left(\cos\dfrac{8\pi}{6}-i\sin\dfrac{8\pi}{6}\right)$.

	Method 2		3
	$\bullet^4$ find w^2 correctly and attempt to find a higher power of w [Note 1]	$\bullet^4$ eg $w^2=a^2\left(2-2i\sqrt{3}\right)$ and $w^3=a^2\left(2-2i\sqrt{3}\right)\times a\left(\sqrt{3}-i\right)$.	
	$\bullet^5$ obtain w^4	$\bullet^5$ $w^4=a^4\left(-8-8i\sqrt{3}\right)$	
	$\bullet^6$ complete expansion and express in form $ka^n\left(x+i\sqrt{y}\right)$	$\bullet^6$ $w^8=128a^8\left(-1+i\sqrt{3}\right)$	

Notes:

1. Accept the omission of 'a' at $\bullet^4$ and $\bullet^5$ provided a^8 appears in the final answer.

	Method 3		3
	$\bullet^4$ write down full binomial expansion[1,2]	$\bullet^4$ $\begin{pmatrix}8\\0\end{pmatrix}\left(\sqrt{3}\right)^8\left(-i\right)^0+\begin{pmatrix}8\\1\end{pmatrix}\left(\sqrt{3}\right)^7\left(-i\right)^1$ $+\begin{pmatrix}8\\2\end{pmatrix}\left(\sqrt{3}\right)^7\left(-i\right)^2...+\begin{pmatrix}8\\8\end{pmatrix}\left(\sqrt{3}\right)^0\left(-i\right)^8$	
	$\bullet^5$ simplifies individual terms	$\bullet^5$ $81-216i\sqrt{3}-756+504i\sqrt{3}$ $+630-168i\sqrt{3}-84+8i\sqrt{3}+1$	
	$\bullet^6$ complete expansion and express in form $ka^n\left(x+i\sqrt{y}\right)$	$\bullet^6$ $w^8=128a^8\left(-1+i\sqrt{3}\right)$	

Notes:
1. For the award of $\bullet^4$ a **full** expansion must be written out.
2. Accept the omission of 'a' at $\bullet^4$ and $\bullet^5$ provided a^8 appears in the final answer.

Question	Generic scheme	Illustrative scheme	Max mark
9.	•[1] know to use integration by parts **and** start process[1,2,3]	•[1] $\dfrac{1}{8}x^8\left(\ln x\right)^2 - \ldots$	6
	•[2] correct choice of functions to differentiate and integrate **AND** application thereof [1,2,3]	•[2] $\ldots -\dfrac{1}{8}\displaystyle\int x^8 \times \dfrac{d}{dx}\left(\left(\ln x\right)^2\right)dx$	
	•[3] differentiate $\left(\ln x\right)^2$ [4]	•[3] $\dfrac{1}{8}x^8\left(\ln x\right)^2 - \dfrac{1}{4}\displaystyle\int x^7\left(\ln x\right)dx$	
	•[4] know to use second application and begin process[1,2,3,4]	•[4] $\ldots -\left[\dfrac{1}{32}x^8\left(\ln x\right) - \dfrac{1}{32}\displaystyle\int x^8\left(\dfrac{1}{x}\right)dx\right]$	
	•[5] complete second application	•[5] $\ldots -\left[\dfrac{1}{32}x^8\left(\ln x\right) - \dfrac{1}{256}x^8\right]$	
	•[6] simplify[5]	•[6] $\dfrac{1}{8}x^8\left(\ln x\right)^2 - \dfrac{1}{32}x^8\left(\ln x\right) + \dfrac{1}{256}x^8 + c$	

Notes:
1. For candidates who attempt to integrate $\left(\ln x\right)^2$ and differentiate x^7 then •[1], •[4] and •[6] may be awarded but not •[2], •[3] and •[5].
2. Evidence of use of integration by parts would be the appearance of an attempt to integrate one term and differentiate the other.
3. For candidates who attempt to substitute for $\ln x$ eg $t = \ln x$ leading to $\int t^2 e^{8t}\, dt$ then

   •[1] becomes available upon evidence of using integration by parts ie. $t^2.\dfrac{1}{8}e^{8t} - \ldots$

   •[6] is only available for a final answer expressed as a function of x.

4. For candidates who incorrectly differentiate $\left(\ln x\right)^2$ and do not require a second application of integration by parts, only •[1], •[2] and •[6] are available.
5. Do not penalise the omission of "$+c$".

Question	Generic scheme	Illustrative scheme	Max mark
10.	•[1] give counterexample	•[1] eg. choose $p = 7$ **COUNTEREXAMPLE** $2(7)+1 = 15$ and since $15 = 5 \times 3$, hence not prime, statement is false	4
	PROOF •[2] set up n [Notes1,2]	**PROOF** •[2] $n = 3a+1,\ a \in \mathbb{N}_0$	
	•[3] consider expansion of n^3 [Note 3]	•[3] $n^3 = 27a^3 + 27a^2 + 9a + 1$	
	•[4] complete proof with conclusion[4]	•[4] $= 3\left(9a^3 + 9a^2 + 3a\right) + 1$ and statement such as "so n^3 has remainder 1 when divided by 3 $\therefore$ statement is true".	

Notes:
1. Do not penalise the omission of $a \in \mathbb{N}_0$ in •[2].
2. Treat a statement such as $n = 3n+1$ as bad form.
3. •[3] can only be awarded for the correct expansion of $\left(3a+1\right)^3$.
4. Minimum statement of conclusion in •[4] is "true".
5. Where a candidate invokes an incorrect use of proof by contradiction full credit may still be available provided all relevant steps are included.

Question	Generic scheme	Illustrative scheme	Max mark
11.	**Method 1**		4
	$\bullet^1$ state differential equation[1,2]	$\bullet^1$ $\dfrac{dh}{dt} = 5$	
	$\bullet^2$ state relationship or apply chain rule[3]	$\bullet^2$ $\dfrac{dV}{dt} = \dfrac{dV}{dh} \cdot \dfrac{dh}{dt}$ $V = h^3$	
	$\bullet^3$ find the rate of change of volume with respect to height[3]	$\bullet^3$ $\dfrac{dV}{dh} = 3h^2$	
	$\bullet^4$ evaluate[4]	$\bullet^4$ $\dfrac{dV}{dt} = 3h^2 \times 5 = 3(3)^2 \times 5 = 135 \text{ cm}^3 \text{ s}^{-1}$	
	Method 2		
	$\bullet^1$ express volume as a function of time	$\bullet^1$ $V = 125t^3$	
	$\bullet^2$ find rate of change of volume with respect to time	$\bullet^2$ $\dfrac{dV}{dt} = 375t^2$	
	$\bullet^3$ find value of t	$\bullet^3$ $t = \dfrac{3}{5}$	
	$\bullet^4$ evaluate	$\bullet^4$ $\dfrac{dV}{dt} = 375\left(\dfrac{3}{5}\right)^2 = 135 \text{ cm}^3 \text{ s}^{-1}$	

Notes:

1. A candidate who assumes that only the height changes — and that the length and breadth are constant — can be awarded $\bullet^1$ and $\bullet^2$ only.
2. Where a candidate uses the wrong formula for the volume of a cube only $\bullet^1$ and $\bullet^2$ are available.
3. A candidate using Method 1 who writes $\dfrac{dV}{dt} = 3h^2 \dfrac{dh}{dt}$ can be awarded $\bullet^2$ and $\bullet^3$.
4. To award $\bullet^4$ there must be evidence of substituting 3 and 5. Correct units must also be included.

Question	Generic scheme	Illustrative scheme	Max mark
12. (a)	•[1] correct shape •[2] graph passes through $2c$ on the positive x- and y-axes	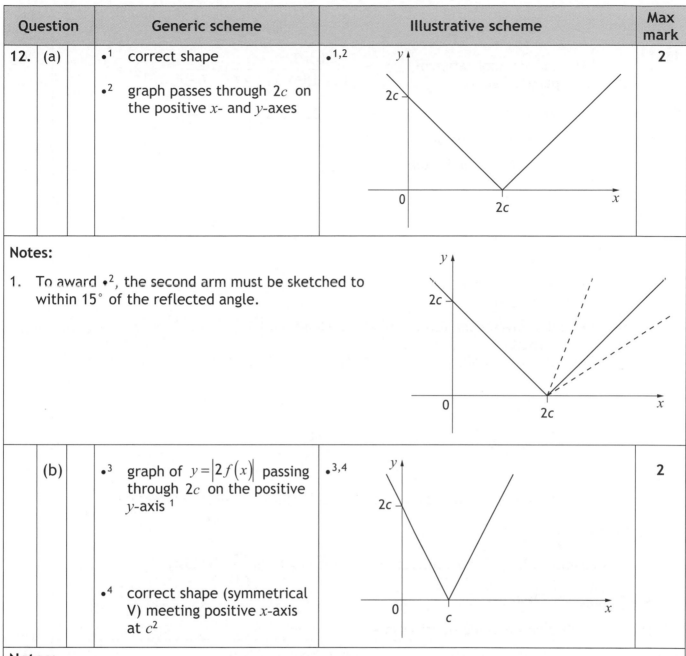	2

Notes:

1. To award •[2], the second arm must be sketched to within $15°$ of the reflected angle.

(b)	•[3] graph of $y=\left\|2f(x)\right\|$ passing through $2c$ on the positive y-axis [1] •[4] correct shape (symmetrical V) meeting positive x-axis at c^2		2

Notes:
1. For a candidate who sketches the graph of $y=2f(x)$ award •[3] for showing a straight line passing through $(0,-2c)$.
2. To award •[4], the second arm must be sketched to within $15°$ of the reflected angle.

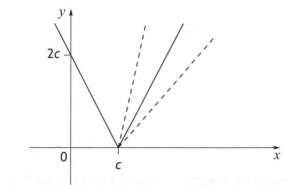

Question			Generic scheme		Illustrative scheme	Max mark
13.		$\bullet^1$	correct application of partial fractions	$\bullet^1$	$\dfrac{3x+32}{(x+4)(6-x)}=\dfrac{A}{x+4}+\dfrac{B}{6-x}$	9
		$\bullet^2$	starts process	$\bullet^2$	$3x+32=A(6-x)+B(x+4)$	
		$\bullet^3$	calculate one value	$\bullet^3$	$A=2$	
		$\bullet^4$	calculate second value	$\bullet^4$	$B=5$	
		$\bullet^5$	re-state integral in partial fractions	$\bullet^5$	$\displaystyle\int_3^4\left(\dfrac{2}{(x+4)}+\dfrac{5}{(6-x)}\right)dx$	
		$\bullet^6$	one term correctly integrated[1]	$\bullet^6$	$\left[2\ln\lvert x+4\rvert\ldots\right.$	
		$\bullet^7$	Integrate second term correctly[1]	$\bullet^7$	$\left.\ldots-5\ln\lvert6-x\rvert\right]_3^4$	
		$\bullet^8$	substitute limits	$\bullet^8$	$\left(2\ln\lvert4+4\rvert-5\ln\lvert6-4\rvert\right)$ $-\left(2\ln\lvert3+4\rvert-5\ln\lvert6-3\rvert\right)$	
		$\bullet^9$	evaluate to expected form[Note 3]	$\bullet^9$	$=\ln\dfrac{486}{49}$	

Notes:
1. Do not penalise lack of modulus signs unless the candidate attempts to integrate $\dfrac{1}{x-6}$ rather than $\dfrac{1}{6-x}$.
2. Award maximum [8/9] for appropriate working leading to $\ln\dfrac{98}{243}$ ($\bullet^9$ lost) or $\ln\dfrac{2048}{11907}$ ($\bullet^7$ lost).
3. Do not penalise unsimplified fractions in $\bullet^9$.

Question			Generic scheme		Illustrative scheme	Max mark
14.	(a)	$\bullet^1$	convert any two components of L_2 to parametric form[1]	$\bullet^1$	two from $x=3-2\mu,$ $y=8+\mu,$ $z=-1+3\mu$	5
		$\bullet^2$	two linear equations involving two distinct parameters	$\bullet^2$	two from $4+3\lambda=3-2\mu,$ $2+4\lambda=8+\mu,$ $-7\lambda=-1+3\mu$	
		$\bullet^3$	find parameter values	$\bullet^3$	$\lambda=1,\ \mu=-2$	
		$\bullet^4$	verify third component in **both** equations or equivalent	$\bullet^4$	eg $z_1=-7\times1$ and $z_2=3(-2)-1$ therefore the lines intersect	
		$\bullet^5$	find point of intersection	$\bullet^5$	$(7,6,-7)$	

Notes:
1. A candidate who uses λ as the second parameter can only be awarded $\bullet^1$ unless this is rectified later in the question.
2. Do not penalise the omission of the statement 'therefore the lines intersect'.

Question	Generic scheme	Illustrative scheme	Max mark
(b)	•[6] identify first direction vector [1,2,3]	•[6] $\mathbf{d}_1 = 3\mathbf{i} + 4\mathbf{j} - 7\mathbf{k}$	**4**
	•[7] identify second direction vector [1,2,3]	•[7] $\mathbf{d}_2 = -2\mathbf{i} + \mathbf{j} + 3\mathbf{k}$	
	•[8] calculate magnitudes and scalar product	•[8] $\lvert\mathbf{d}_1\rvert = \sqrt{74},\ \lvert\mathbf{d}_2\rvert = \sqrt{14}$ and $\mathbf{d}_1 \cdot \mathbf{d}_2 = -6 + 4 - 21 = -23$	
	•[9] calculate obtuse angle [4,5]	•[9] $\cos^{-1}\left(\dfrac{-23}{\sqrt{74}\sqrt{14}}\right) \approx 135 \cdot 6^\circ$	

Notes:
1. For $L_1 = 3\mathbf{i} + 4\mathbf{j} - 7\mathbf{k}$ and $L_2 = -2\mathbf{i} + \mathbf{j} + 3\mathbf{k}$ or equivalent, lose •[6] but •[7] is available (repeated error).
2. Do not penalise $\mathbf{L}_1 = 3\mathbf{i} + 4\mathbf{j} - 7\mathbf{k}$ and $\mathbf{L}_2 = -2\mathbf{i} + \mathbf{j} + 3\mathbf{k}$.
3. For $L_1 : 3\mathbf{i} + 4\mathbf{j} - 7\mathbf{k}$ and $L_2 : -2\mathbf{i} + \mathbf{j} + 3\mathbf{k}$ or equivalent, •[6] and •[7] are both available.
4. For the award of •[9] accept 136°.
5. •[9] is not available to candidates who calculate an obtuse angle correctly but who subsequently calculate an acute angle.

15.		•[1] state auxiliary equation[1]	•[1] $m^2 + 5m + 6 = 0$ $m = -3,\ m = -2$	**10**
		•[2] solve auxiliary equation and state complementary function[2,3]	•[2] $y = Ae^{-3x} + Be^{-2x}$	
		•[3] construct particular integral	•[3] $y = Cx^2 + Dx + E$	
		•[4] differentiate particular integral	•[4] $\dfrac{dy}{dx} = 2Cx + D$ and $\dfrac{d^2 y}{dx^2} = 2C$	
		•[5] calculate one coefficient of the particular integral	•[5] $C = 2$	
		•[6] calculate remaining coefficients	•[6] $D = -3, E = 1$ $y = Ae^{-3x} + Be^{-2x} + 2x^2 - 3x + 1$	
		•[7] differentiate general solution[3]	•[7] $\dfrac{dy}{dx} = -3Ae^{-3x} - 2Be^{-2x} + 4x - 3$	
		•[8] construct equations using given conditions	•[8] $A + B = -7$ and $3A + 2B = -6$ or equivalent	
		•[9] Find one coefficient	•[9] $A = 8$ or $B = -15$	
		•[10] Find other coefficient **and** state particular solution	•[10] $y = 8e^{-3x} - 15e^{-2x} + 2x^2 - 3x + 1$	

Notes:
1. For •[1] do not penalise the omission of '$= 0$'.
2. •[2] can be awarded if the Complementary Function appears later as part of the general solution, as opposed to being explicitly stated immediately after solving the Auxiliary Equation.
3. A candidate who obtains $m = 2$ and $m = 3$ from a correct auxiliary equation, leading to $y = 20e^{3x} - 27e^{2x} + 2x^2 - 3x + 1$ cannot gain •[2] but all other marks are available.
4. Where a candidate substitutes the given conditions into the Complementary Function to obtain values of A and B and then finds the particular integral correctly •[8] and •[9] are unavailable.

Question	Generic scheme	Illustrative scheme	Max mark
16.	**Method 1** — working in minutes ($t=0$ at noon)		9
	$\bullet^1$ construct integral equation Note 1	$\bullet^1$ $\int \frac{1}{(T-T_F)} dT = \int -k\,dt$	
	$\bullet^2$ integrate[2]	$\bullet^2$ $\ln(T-T_F) = -kt+c$	
	$\bullet^3$ find constant, c	$\bullet^3$ $\ln(9\cdot 8-4) = -k(0)+c$ $c = \ln 5\cdot 8$	
	$\bullet^4$ substitute using given information[4]	$\bullet^4$ $\ln(6\cdot 5-4) = -15k + \ln 5\cdot 8$	
	$\bullet^5$ find constant, k	$\bullet^5$ $k = \frac{\ln 2\cdot 5 - \ln 5\cdot 8}{-15} = 0\cdot 05610...$	
	$\bullet^6$ substitute given condition	$\bullet^6$ $\ln(25-4) = -0\cdot 05610...t + \ln 5\cdot 8$	
	$\bullet^7$ know how to find time	$\bullet^7$ $t = \frac{\ln 21 - \ln 5\cdot 8}{-0\cdot 05610...}$	
	$\bullet^8$ calculate time	$\bullet^8$ $t = -22\cdot 93...$	
	$\bullet^9$ state the time to the nearest minute[3]	$\bullet^9$ The liquid was placed in the fridge at 11:37 (am)	
	Method 2 — working in minutes ($t=0$ when $T=25$)		
	$\bullet^1$ construct integral equation Note 1	$\bullet^1$ $\int \frac{1}{(T-T_F)} dT = \int -k\,dt$	
	$\bullet^2$ integrate[2]	$\bullet^2$ $\ln(T-T_F) = -kt+c$	
	$\bullet^3$ find constant, c.	$\bullet^3$ $\ln(25-4) = -k(0)+c,$ $c = \ln 21$	
	$\bullet^4$ substitute using given information	$\bullet^4$ $\ln(9\cdot 8-4) = -k(t) + \ln 21$	
	$\bullet^5$ know to use $t+15$ Note 5	$\bullet^5$ appearance of $(t+15)$	
	$\bullet^6$ use given condition	$\bullet^6$ $\ln(6\cdot 5-4) = -k(t+15) + \ln 21$	
	$\bullet^7$ find constant, k Note 6	$\bullet^7$ $k = -\frac{1}{15}\ln\left(\frac{2\cdot 5}{5\cdot 8}\right) = 0\cdot 05610...$	
	$\bullet^8$ calculate time	$\bullet^8$ $t = \ln\left(\frac{21}{5\cdot 8}\right) \div 0\cdot 05610... = 22\cdot 93$	
	$\bullet^9$ state the time to the nearest minute[3]	$\bullet^9$ The liquid was placed in the fridge at 11:37 (am).	

Question	Generic scheme	Illustrative scheme	Max mark
	Method 3 — working in hours ($t = 0$ at midnight)		
	$\bullet^1$ construct integral equation [Note 1]	$\bullet^1 \quad \displaystyle\int \frac{1}{(T - T_F)} dT = \int -k\, dt$	
	$\bullet^2$ integrate [2]	$\bullet^2 \quad \ln(T - T_F) = -kt + c$	
	$\bullet^3$ use initial conditions	$\bullet^3 \quad \ln 5 \cdot 8 = -12k + c$	
	$\bullet^4$ interpret later time	$\bullet^4 \quad \ln 2 \cdot 5 = -12 \cdot 25k + c$	
	$\bullet^5$ find constant, k	$\bullet^5 \quad \ln 5 \cdot 8 - \ln 2 \cdot 5 = 0 \cdot 25 k$ $\qquad k = 3 \cdot 366\ldots$	
	$\bullet^6$ find the constant, c	$\bullet^6 \quad \ln(9 \cdot 8 - 4) = -3 \cdot 366\ldots \times 12 + c$ $\qquad c = 42 \cdot 15\ldots$	
	$\bullet^7$ know to find time	$\bullet^7 \quad \ln(25 - 4) = -3 \cdot 366\ldots t + 42 \cdot 15$	
	$\bullet^8$ calculate time	$\bullet^8 \quad t = \dfrac{42 \cdot 15 - \ln 21}{3 \cdot 366\ldots}$ $\qquad = 11 \cdot 62\ldots$	
	$\bullet^9$ state the time to the nearest minute [3]	$\bullet^9$ The liquid was placed in the fridge at 11:37 (am).	
	Method 4 — working in minutes ($t = 0$ when $T = 25$)		
	$\bullet^1$ construct integral equation [Note 1]	$\bullet^1 \quad \displaystyle\int \frac{1}{(T - T_F)} dT = \int -k\, dt$	
	$\bullet^2$ integrate [2]	$\bullet^2 \quad \ln(T - T_F) = -kt + c$ $\qquad T - T_F = e^{-kt + c}$ $\qquad T = Ae^{-kt} + T_F$ $\qquad T = Ae^{-kt} + 4$	
	$\bullet^3$ use initial condition to calculate A	$\bullet^3 \quad 25 = Ae^{-k(0)} + 4 \therefore A = 21$	
	$\bullet^4$ substitute using given information	$\bullet^4 \quad 9 \cdot 8 = 21e^{-kt} + 4$	
	$\bullet^5$ know to use $t + 15$ [Note 7]	$\bullet^5$ appearance of $(t + 15)$	
	$\bullet^6$ substitute using given information	$\bullet^6 \quad 6 \cdot 5 = 21e^{-k(t+15)} + 4$	
	$\bullet^7$ find constant, k	$\bullet^7 \quad k = \dfrac{\ln\left(\dfrac{5 \cdot 8}{21}\right) - \ln\left(\dfrac{2 \cdot 5}{21}\right)}{15} = 0 \cdot 0561\ldots$	
	$\bullet^8$ calculate time	$\bullet^8 \quad t = \ln\left(\dfrac{21}{5 \cdot 8}\right) \div 0 \cdot 05610\ldots = 22 \cdot 93\ldots$	
	$\bullet^9$ state the time to the nearest minute [3]	$\bullet^9$ The liquid was placed in the fridge at 11:37 (am).	

Question	Generic scheme	Illustrative scheme	Max mark

Notes

General note:

Many candidates may use a combination of the given methods. For all methods the evidence for $\bullet^1$, $\bullet^2$, $\bullet^8$ and $\bullet^9$ is the same. To award $\bullet^3$ up to $\bullet^7$ note that:

  two marks are awarded for using two different values of T

  one mark is awarded for finding the constant of integration

  one mark is awarded for finding or eliminating k (refer to Note **6**)

  one mark is awarded for dealing with the elapsed time (noon until 12:15)

1. Do not penalise the omission of integral symbols at $\bullet^1$. (All Methods)
2. Do not penalise omission of "$+c$" at $\bullet^2$. However, it is necessary to access some later marks. (All Methods)
3. Where a candidate obtains an incorrect final answer because of earlier rounding, only $\bullet^9$ is unavailable. (All Methods)
4. For Method 1, if the candidate works in hours:

  $\bullet^4$ $\ln(6\cdot5-4)=-0\cdot25k+\ln(5\cdot8)$

  $\bullet^5$ $k=-4(\ln2\cdot5-\ln5\cdot8)=3\cdot366...$

  $\bullet^6$ $\ln(25-4)=-3\cdot366...t+\ln5\cdot8$

  $\bullet^7$ $t=\dfrac{\ln21-\ln5\cdot8}{-3\cdot366...}$

  $\bullet^8$ $t=-0\cdot3822...$

5. For Method 2, if the candidate works in hours:

  $\bullet^5$ appearance of $(t+0\cdot25)$

  $\bullet^6$ $\ln(6\cdot5-4)=-k(t+0\cdot25)+\ln21$

  $\bullet^7$ $k=-\dfrac{1}{0\cdot25}\ln\left(\dfrac{2\cdot5}{5\cdot8}\right)=3\cdot366...$

  $\bullet^8$ $t=\ln\left(\dfrac{21}{5\cdot8}\right)\div0\cdot366...=0\cdot3822...$

6. In Method 2 $\bullet^7$ can be awarded for eliminating k.

7. For Method 4, if the candidate works in hours:

  $\bullet^5$ appearance of $(t+0\cdot25)$

  $\bullet^6$ $6\cdot5=21e^{-k(t+0\cdot25)}+4$

  $\bullet^7$ $k=\dfrac{\ln\left(\dfrac{5\cdot8}{21}\right)-\ln\left(\dfrac{2\cdot5}{21}\right)}{0\cdot25}=3\cdot366...$

  $\bullet^8$ $t=\ln\left(\dfrac{21}{5\cdot8}\right)\div3\cdot366...=0\cdot3822...$

ADVANCED HIGHER MATHEMATICS 2017

Question	Generic scheme	Illustrative scheme	Max mark
1.	$\bullet^1$ write down binomial expansion [1,3,4]	$\bullet^1$ $= \begin{pmatrix} 3 \\ 0 \end{pmatrix}\left(\dfrac{2}{y^2}\right)^3 + \begin{pmatrix} 3 \\ 1 \end{pmatrix}\left(\dfrac{2}{y^2}\right)^2(-5y)$ $+\begin{pmatrix} 3 \\ 2 \end{pmatrix}\left(\dfrac{2}{y^2}\right)(-5y)^2 + \begin{pmatrix} 3 \\ 3 \end{pmatrix}(-5y)^3$	4
	$\bullet^2$ resolve signs [3,4]		
	$\bullet^3$ simplify coefficients or powers of y [2,4]		
	$\bullet^4$ complete simplification and obtain expression [2,4,5,6]	$\bullet^{2,3,4}$ $\dfrac{8}{y^6} - \dfrac{60}{y^3} + 150 - 125y^3$	

Notes:
1. Accept any correct form for binomial coefficients.
2. Accept negative powers of y.
3. For candidates who expand $\left(\dfrac{2}{y^2} + 5y\right)^3$ using the Binomial Theorem $\bullet^1$ and $\bullet^2$ are not available.
4. Candidates who expand $\left(\dfrac{2}{y^2} - 5y\right)^3$ without using the Binomial Theorem may be awarded $\bullet^2$, $\bullet^3$ and $\bullet^4$ but $\bullet^1$ is not available.
5. $\bullet^4$ is not available for a final expression which contains the term '$150y^0$'.
6. Do not award $\bullet^4$ where the candidate produces incorrect working subsequent to a correct simplification.

Question	Generic scheme	Illustrative scheme	Max mark
2.	$\bullet^1$ state expression	$\bullet^1$ $\dfrac{x^2-6x+20}{(x+1)(x-2)^2} = \dfrac{A}{(x+1)} + \dfrac{B}{(x-2)} + \dfrac{C}{(x-2)^2}$	4
	$\bullet^2$ form equation	$\bullet^2$ $x^2-6x+20 = A(x-2)^2 + B(x+1)(x-2) + C(x+1)$	
	$\bullet^3$ obtain two of A, B and C	$\bullet^3$ $A=3,\ B=-2,\ C=4$	
	$\bullet^4$ obtain final constant and state expression [1]	$\bullet^4$ $\dfrac{3}{(x+1)} - \dfrac{2}{(x-2)} + \dfrac{4}{(x-2)^2}$	

Notes:
1. At $\bullet^4$ accept $\dfrac{3}{(x+1)} + \dfrac{-2}{(x-2)} + \dfrac{4}{(x-2)^2}$ but do not accept $\dfrac{3}{(x+1)} + -\dfrac{2}{(x-2)} + \dfrac{4}{(x-2)^2}$.

Question	Generic scheme	Illustrative scheme	Max mark
3.	$\bullet^1$ evidence use of quotient rule with one term of numerator correct	$\bullet^1$ $2xe^{x^2-1}(x^2-1) - \ldots$	3
	$\bullet^2$ complete differentiation	$\bullet^2$ $\dfrac{\ldots 2xe^{x^2-1}}{(x^2-1)^2}$	
	$\bullet^3$ simplify [1,2,3]	$\bullet^3$ $\dfrac{2xe^{x^2-1}(x^2-2)}{(x^2-1)^2}$	

Question	Generic scheme	Illustrative scheme	Max mark

Notes:

1. At $\bullet^3$ accept $\dfrac{2x^3 e^{x^2-1} - 4xe^{x^2-1}}{\left(x^2-1\right)^2}$ but not accept $\dfrac{2xe^{x^2-1}\left(\left(x^2-1\right)-1\right)}{\left(x^2-1\right)^2}$ (GM Principle (l)).

2. Do not award $\bullet^3$ where the candidate produces further incorrect simplification subsequent to a correct answer.

3. Where a candidate differentiates incorrectly $\bullet^3$ may be available provided like terms are collected in the numerator. Where this is not possible the expression should be fully factorised (this need not extend to exponential functions of differing powers). Where no simplification is possible $\bullet^3$ is not available.

Question	Generic scheme	Illustrative scheme	Max mark
4. (a)	$\bullet^1$ evidence use of valid strategy	$\bullet^1$ e.g. $a+4d=-6$ $a+11d=-34$	2
	$\bullet^2$ obtain values of a and d [1]	$\bullet^2$ $a=10, d=-4$	

Notes:

1. Candidates who state correct values for both a and d without working may be awarded $\bullet^1$ and $\bullet^2$.

Question	Generic scheme	Illustrative scheme	Max mark
(b)	$\bullet^3$ set up equation	$\bullet^3$ $\dfrac{n}{2}\left[20-4\left(n-1\right)\right]=-144$	3
	$\bullet^4$ rearrange to standard form [1]	$\bullet^4$ $2n^2-12n-144=0$	
	$\bullet^5$ determine the value of n [2]	$\bullet^5$ $n>0 \therefore n=12$	

Notes:

1. $\bullet^4$ may be awarded only where a quadratic equation has been expressed in standard form.
2. $\bullet^5$ may be awarded only where an invalid solution for n has been discarded.

Question	Generic scheme	Illustrative scheme	Max mark
5. (a) (i)	$\bullet^1$ set up augmented matrix	$\bullet^1$ $\begin{pmatrix} 1 & 2 & -1 & \vdots & -3 \\ 4 & -2 & 3 & \vdots & 11 \\ 3 & 1 & 2\lambda & \vdots & 8 \end{pmatrix}$	4
	$\bullet^2$ obtain two zeros [1]	$\bullet^2$ $\begin{pmatrix} 1 & 2 & -1 & \vdots & -3 \\ 0 & -10 & 7 & \vdots & 23 \\ 0 & -5 & 2\lambda+3 & \vdots & 17 \end{pmatrix}$	
	$\bullet^3$ complete row operations [1]	$\bullet^3$ $\begin{pmatrix} 1 & 2 & -1 & \vdots & -3 \\ 0 & -10 & 7 & \vdots & 23 \\ 0 & 0 & 4\lambda-1 & \vdots & 11 \end{pmatrix}$	
	$\bullet^4$ obtain expression for z [2,3]	$\bullet^4$ $z=\dfrac{11}{4\lambda-1}$	
(ii)	$\bullet^5$ state value of λ	$\bullet^5$ $\lambda=\dfrac{1}{4}$	1
(b)	$\bullet^6$ find solution [4]	$\bullet^6$ $z=-1, y=-3, x=2$	1

Notes:

1. Only Gaussian Elimination (i.e. a systematic approach using EROs) is acceptable for the award of $\bullet^2$ and $\bullet^3$.

2. Do not accept an answer of $\left(4\lambda-1\right)z=11$ when awarding $\bullet^4$.

3. At $\bullet^4$ accept an unsimplified expression for z e.g. $z=\dfrac{5\cdot5}{2\lambda-\frac{1}{2}}$.

4. Where decimal approximations are used $\bullet^6$ is available only where candidates work to 3sf or better.

Question			Generic scheme	Illustrative scheme	Max mark
6.			•[1] differentiate $5x^2$	•[1] $\dfrac{du}{dx}=10x$ or $du=10x\,dx$	6
			•[2] find limits for u [3]	•[2] $u=0, u=\dfrac{1}{2}$	
			•[3] replace '$x\,dx$' [1,2]	•[3] $\dfrac{1}{10}\displaystyle\int ...du$	
			•[4] obtain integrand [1,2]	•[4] $\dfrac{1}{10}\displaystyle\int_0^{\frac{1}{2}}\dfrac{1}{\sqrt{1-u^2}}\,du$	
			•[5] integrate [2,3,4,5]	•[5] $\dfrac{1}{10}\Big[\sin^{-1}u\Big]_0^{\frac{1}{2}}$	
			•[6] evaluate [2,6,7,8]	•[6] $\dfrac{\pi}{60}$	

Notes:
1. At •[3] and •[4] treat as bad form situations where candidates either omit limits or retain limits for x.
2. Where candidates attempt to integrate an expression containing both u and x, where x is either inside the integrand or erroneously taken outside as a constant, only •[1] and •[2] may be available.
3. Where candidates do not change limits but who produce working leading to $\dfrac{1}{10}\Big[\sin^{-1}\big(5x^2\big)\Big]_0^{\frac{1}{\sqrt{10}}}$, •[2] may be awarded.
4. Where candidates show no working but write down $\dfrac{1}{10}\Big[\sin^{-1}\big(5x^2\big)\Big]_0^{\frac{1}{\sqrt{10}}}$, •[1] is not available.
5. •[5] and •[6] are unavailable to candidates who having been awarded •[4] subsequently proceed to $\dfrac{1}{10}\left[\dfrac{\big(1-u^2\big)^{\frac{1}{2}}}{-\frac{1}{2}\times 2u}\right]$.
6. For candidates who integrate incorrectly, •[6] may be available provided division by zero does not occur.
7. For candidates who, upon integrating, obtain a trigonometric expression and then work in degrees •[6] is unavailable.
8. Disregard the appearance of a decimal approximation subsequent to a simplified exact value.

Question			Generic scheme	Illustrative scheme	Max mark
7.	(a)	(i)	•[1] determine value of x	•[1] $x=8$	1
		(ii)	•[2] find inverse [1]	•[2] $P^{-1}=\dfrac{1}{2}\begin{pmatrix} -1 & -2 \\ 5 & 8 \end{pmatrix}$	1
		(iii)	•[3] state transpose	•[3] $Q'=\begin{pmatrix} 2 & 4 \\ -3 & y \end{pmatrix}$	2
			•[4] obtain product [2,3]	•[4] $P^{-1}Q'=\begin{pmatrix} 2 & -2-y \\ -7 & 10+4y \end{pmatrix}$	

Notes:
1. At •[2] accept $P^{-1}=\dfrac{1}{2}\begin{pmatrix} -1 & -2 \\ 5 & x \end{pmatrix}$.

2. For •[4] accept $P^{-1}Q'=\dfrac{1}{2}\begin{pmatrix} 4 & -4-2y \\ -14 & 20+8y \end{pmatrix}$ but not $P^{-1}Q'=\dfrac{1}{2}\begin{pmatrix} -2+6 & -4-2y \\ 10-24 & 20+8y \end{pmatrix}$.

3. •[4] may be awarded only where y is present.

Question			Generic scheme		Illustrative scheme		Max mark
	(b)		$\bullet^5$ state condition for singularity [1,2]	$\bullet^5$	$\det R = 0$ or one row is a multiple of the other		2
			$\bullet^6$ obtain value for z [2]	$\bullet^6$	$z = 15$		

Notes:
1. $\det R = 0$ may be stated or implied in the working for $\bullet^6$.
2. For an answer of $z = 15$ without justification, $\bullet^5$ is not available.

8.			$\bullet^1$ start process	$\bullet^1$	$1595 = 1 \times 1218 + 377$		4
			$\bullet^2$ obtain remainder of 29 [1]	$\bullet^2$	$1218 = 3 \times 377 + 87$ $377 = 4 \times 87 + 29$ $87 = 3 \times 29 + 0$		
			$\bullet^3$ express gcd in terms of 377 and 1218	$\bullet^3$	$29 = 377 - 4(1218 - 3 \times 377)$		
			$\bullet^4$ state values of a and b [2]	$\bullet^4$	$a = 13, b = -17$		

Notes:
1. At $\bullet^2$ the gcd does not need to be explicitly stated.
2. The minimum requirement for $\bullet^4$ is $1595 \times 13 + 1218 \times (-17) = 29$.

9.			$\bullet^1$ separate variables and write down integral equation [1,7]	$\bullet^1$	$\int \dfrac{dy}{1+y^2} = \int e^{2x}\, dx$		5
			$\bullet^2$ integrate LHS [2]	$\bullet^2$	$\tan^{-1} y$		
			$\bullet^3$ integrate RHS [3]	$\bullet^3$	$\dfrac{1}{2} e^{2x} + c$		
			$\bullet^4$ evaluate constant of integration [2,3,4,5]	$\bullet^4$	$c = \dfrac{\pi}{4} - \dfrac{1}{2}$		
			$\bullet^5$ express y in terms of x [3,5,6]	$\bullet^5$	$y = \tan\left(\dfrac{1}{2} e^{2x} + \dfrac{\pi}{4} - \dfrac{1}{2}\right)$		

Notes:
1. Do not withhold $\bullet^1$ where dy and dx have been omitted.
2. For candidates who integrate the LHS and obtain a logarithmic expression, $\bullet^2$ and $\bullet^4$ are not available.
3. For candidates who omit a constant of integration, $\bullet^3$ may be awarded but $\bullet^4$ and $\bullet^5$ are unavailable.
4. At $\bullet^4$ accept a decimal value for the constant of integration correct to at least 3sf ($0 \cdot 285$).
5. For candidates who work in degrees, $\bullet^4$ is unavailable but $\bullet^5$ may be awarded.
6. At $\bullet^5$ do not accept e.g. $y = \tan\left(\dfrac{1}{2} e^{2x}\right) + \dfrac{\pi}{4} - \dfrac{1}{2}$, $y = \tan \dfrac{1}{2} e^{2x} + \dfrac{\pi}{4} - \dfrac{1}{2}$.
7. Candidates who use either Integration by Parts or the Integrating Factor Method receive 0/5.

10.	(a)		$\bullet^1$ substitute formulae	$\bullet^1$	$\displaystyle\sum_{r=1}^{n}\left(r^2 + \dfrac{1}{3}r\right) = \dfrac{n(n+1)(2n+1)}{6} + \dfrac{1}{3}\left(\dfrac{n(n+1)}{2}\right)$ $= \dfrac{n(n+1)((2n+1)+1)}{6}$		2
			$\bullet^2$ factorise fully [1]	$\bullet^2$	$= \dfrac{n(n+1)^2}{3}$		

Question	Generic scheme	Illustrative scheme	Max mark

Notes:
1. At $\bullet^2$ do not accept $\dfrac{n(n+1)(n+1)}{3}$ or $\dfrac{2n(n+1)^2}{6}$.

					2
	(b)	$\bullet^3$ substitute $2p$ and 9	$\bullet^3$ $\dfrac{2p(2p+1)^2}{3}$ and $\dfrac{9(9+1)^2}{3}$ $\dfrac{2p(2p+1)^2}{3} - \dfrac{9(9+1)^2}{3}$		
		$\bullet^4$ obtain expression	$\bullet^4$ $= \dfrac{2p(2p+1)^2}{3} - 300$		

11.		**Method 1** $\bullet^1$ take logarithms of both sides and apply rule [1] $\bullet^2$ differentiate LHS $\bullet^3$ evidence use of product rule and one term correct [2] $\bullet^4$ complete differentiation [2] $\bullet^5$ write $\dfrac{dy}{dx}$ in terms of x	$\bullet^1$ $\ln y = (2x^3+1)\ln x$ $\bullet^2$ $\dfrac{1}{y}\dfrac{dy}{dx}$ $\bullet^3$ $6x^2\ln x$ or $\dfrac{2x^3+1}{x}$ $\bullet^4$ $6x^2\ln x + \dfrac{2x^3+1}{x}$ $\bullet^5$ $\dfrac{dy}{dx} = x^{2x^3+1}\left(6x^2\ln x + \dfrac{2x^3+1}{x}\right)$	5

Notes:
1. Accept 'log' in lieu of 'ln'.
2. For candidates who do not attempt to use the product rule, $\bullet^3$ and $\bullet^4$ are not available.

12.	(a)	$\bullet^1$ show half-turn symmetry and indicate $(1,2)$ [1,2] $\bullet^2$ demonstrate graph approaching parallel asymptote through $(0,3)$ [3,4]	$\bullet^{1,2}$ 	2

Notes:
1. To award $\bullet^1$ the candidate's graph should exhibit a smooth change in concavity at the origin.
2. Evidence of $(1,2)$ may appear in (b).
3. At $\bullet^2$ accept $y = \dfrac{1}{2}x + 3$ in lieu of $(0,3)$.
4. Where a candidate's graph diverges from the asymptote in quadrant 1, $\bullet^2$ is not available.
5. For Graph 1 in the Commonly Observed Responses $\bullet^1$, $\bullet^2$, $\bullet^3$ and $\bullet^4$ are not available.
6. For Graph 2 in the Commonly Observed Responses $\bullet^1$, $\bullet^2$ and $\bullet^3$ are not available but $\bullet^4$ may be available where a second asymptote appears in (b).

Question			Generic scheme	Illustrative scheme	Max mark
12.	(b)		•[3] apply modulus function to graph obtained in (a) [1,4]	•[3,4]	2
			•[4] illustrate asymptotes meeting on the y-axis [1,2,3]		

Notes:
1. To receive any credit, a candidate's graph from (a) must have a section lying in quadrant 1.
2. •[4] is still available where a candidate's graph diverges from the asymptotes.
3. At •[4] disregard the application of the modulus function to asymptotes.
4. Showing the image points is not required at •[3].

	(c)		**State the range of values of $f'(x)$ given that $f'(0)=2$.**		
			•[5] state range [1,2,3]	•[5] $\dfrac{1}{2} < f'(x) \le 2$	1

Notes:
1. Do not accept $\dfrac{1}{2} \le f'(x) \le 2$ or $\dfrac{1}{2} < f'(x) < 2$.
2. Accept '$f'(x) > \dfrac{1}{2}$ and $f'(x) \le 2$' but not '$f'(x) > \dfrac{1}{2}$ or $f'(x) \le 2$'.
3. Accept '$f'(x)$ is greater than $\dfrac{1}{2}$ and $f'(x)$ is less than or equal to 2'. Do not accept '$f'(x)$ is between $\dfrac{1}{2}$ and 2'.

13.			•[1] write down contrapositive statement [1,2,7,8]	•[1] The contrapositive of the original statement is: If n is odd then n^2 is odd	4
			•[2] write down appropriate form for n [3,4,7]	•[2] $n = 2k+1,\ k \in \mathbb{Z}$	
			•[3] show n^2 is odd [5,6,7]	•[3] $n^2 = 2(2k^2+2k)+1$ which is odd	
			•[4] communicate	•[4] contrapositive statement is true therefore original statement is true	

Question	Generic scheme	Illustrative scheme	Max mark

Notes:

1. A candidate who incorrectly states the contrapositive as n^2 is odd $\Rightarrow n$ is odd (or any other statement masquerading as the contrapositive) and subsequently demonstrates that when n is odd then n^2 is odd may be awarded $\bullet^3$ only.

2. The minimum requirement for $\bullet^1$ is a statement such as:

    n is odd $\Rightarrow n^2$ is odd

    n is odd then n^2 is odd

    n is odd is a sufficient condition for n^2 is odd

    n is odd only if n^2 is odd

    n^2 is odd when n is odd

    Do not accept "n is odd, n^2 is odd" or "n is odd when n^2 is odd

3. At $\bullet^2$ $k \in \mathbb{Z}$ is not required. Accept the form $n = 2k \pm a$, where a is a specified odd number.

4. For candidates who proceed from:

e.g.	$n = 2n + 1$	$\bullet^2$ and $\bullet^4$ are not available
e.g.	$n = 2k$	$\bullet^2$, $\bullet^3$ and $\bullet^4$ are not available
e.g.	$n = k + 1$	$\bullet^2$, $\bullet^3$ and $\bullet^4$ are not available (n is not always odd)
e.g.	$n = 4k + 1$	$\bullet^2$ is not available (not all odd numbers covered by this form)

5. At $\bullet^3$ accept $n^2 = 4(\ldots) + 1$, $n^2 = 2k(\ldots) + 1$ or $n^2 = 4k(\ldots) + 1$.

6. At $\bullet^3$ candidates must state a conclusion e.g. "which is odd".

7. Candidates who carry out a proof by contradiction may be awarded $\bullet^2$ and $\bullet^3$ only.

8. Candidates who write $\neg Q \Rightarrow \neg P$ may be awarded $\bullet^1$ where they either identify P and Q or have written $P \Rightarrow Q$.

Question			Generic scheme	Illustrative scheme	Max mark
14.			$\bullet^1$ construct auxiliary equation [1,9]	$\bullet^1$ $m^2 - 6m + 9 = 0$	10
			$\bullet^2$ solve auxiliary equation and state CF [2,3,4,5,6,7,9]	$\bullet^2$ $y = Ae^{3x} + Bxe^{3x}$	
			$\bullet^3$ state PI	$\bullet^3$ $y = C\sin x + D\cos x$ $\dfrac{dy}{dx} = C\cos x - D\sin x$	
			$\bullet^4$ obtain first and second derivatives of PI	$\bullet^4$ $\dfrac{d^2y}{dx^2} = -C\sin x - D\cos x$	
			$\bullet^5$ substitute	$\bullet^5$ $-C\sin x - D\cos x$ $-6(C\cos x - D\sin x)$ $+9(C\sin x + D\cos x) = 8\sin x + 19\cos x$	
			$\bullet^6$ derive equations	$\bullet^6$ $8C + 6D = 8$ $-6C + 8D = 19$	
			$\bullet^7$ obtain both constants of PI	$\bullet^7$ $C = -\dfrac{1}{2}, D = 2$	
			$\bullet^8$ differentiate general solution [5,6,7,9,10]	$\bullet^8$ $\dfrac{dy}{dx} = 3Ae^{3x} + Be^{3x} + 3Bxe^{3x} - \dfrac{1}{2}\cos x - 2\sin x$	
			$\bullet^9$ determine first constant of general solution [7,8,9]	$\bullet^9$ $A = 5$ or $B = -14$	
			$\bullet^{10}$ determine second constant and state particular solution [3,7,9,10]	$\bullet^{10}$ $y = 5e^{3x} - 14xe^{3x} - \dfrac{1}{2}\sin x + 2\cos x$	

Question	Generic scheme	Illustrative scheme	Max mark

Notes:

1. $\bullet^1$ is not available where '$=0$' has been omitted.
2. $\bullet^2$ can be awarded if the Complementary Function appears later as part of the general solution, as opposed to being explicitly stated immediately after solving the Auxiliary Equation.
3. Do not penalise the omission of '$y = \ldots$' provided it appears at $\bullet^{10}$.
4. For candidates who obtain a CF of $y = Ae^{-3x} + Bxe^{-3x}$ only $\bullet^2$ is not available. In this case the particular solution is $y = 5e^{-3x} + 16xe^{-3x} - \dfrac{1}{2}\sin x + 2\cos x$.
5. For candidates who obtain two real and distinct roots $\bullet^2$ and $\bullet^8$ are not available.
6. For candidates who obtain roots of the form $p \pm qi$: if $p = 0$ and $q \neq 1$ $\bullet^2$ and $\bullet^8$ are not available, otherwise only $\bullet^2$ is not available.
7. For candidates who obtain a CF of $y = Ae^{3x} + Be^{3x}$, $\bullet^2$, $\bullet^8$, $\bullet^9$ and $\bullet^{10}$ are not available.
8. Where a candidate substitutes the given conditions into the CF to obtain values of A and B and then finds the PI correctly, $\bullet^9$ is not available.
9. Where a candidate does not find a PI only $\bullet^1$, $\bullet^2$, $\bullet^8$, $\bullet^9$ and $\bullet^{10}$ are available.
10. Where an error in the differentiation of the general solution results in the value of B being unobtainable then $\bullet^{10}$ is not available.

Question	Generic scheme	Illustrative scheme	Max mark
15. (a)	$\bullet^1$ obtain direction vector [1,2,4] $\bullet^2$ state parametric equations [3,4,5]	$\bullet^1$ $\mathbf{d} = \begin{pmatrix} 2 \\ 6 \\ -1 \end{pmatrix}$ or multiple thereof $\bullet^2$ $\begin{aligned} x &= 2\lambda + 7 \\ y &= 6\lambda + 8 \\ z &= -\lambda + 1 \end{aligned}$ or $\begin{aligned} x &= 2\lambda - 3 \\ y &= 6\lambda - 22 \\ z &= -\lambda + 6 \end{aligned}$ Or equivalent	2

Notes:

1. For candidates who express the equation in either symmetric or vector form $\bullet^1$ is available for evidence of a correct direction vector; $\bullet^2$ is unavailable unless parametric equations appear at (c).
2. Throughout the question accept horizontal vector notation e.g. $(2, 6, -1)$.
3. A correct answer with no working receives full marks.
4. For an incorrect answer containing the correct direction vector but with no working, $\bullet^1$ is available.
5. For an answer with an incorrect direction vector and no working neither $\bullet^1$ nor $\bullet^2$ are available.

Question			Generic scheme		Illustrative scheme	Max mark
(b)		$\bullet^3$	identify vectors	$\bullet^3$	any two from $\overrightarrow{PQ}=\begin{pmatrix}-1\\1\\-2\end{pmatrix}$, $\overrightarrow{PR}=\begin{pmatrix}-5\\6\\-8\end{pmatrix}$, $\overrightarrow{QR}=\begin{pmatrix}-4\\5\\-6\end{pmatrix}$ or equivalent	4
		$\bullet^4$	evidence of strategy for finding normal [1]	$\bullet^4$	$\overrightarrow{PQ}\times\overrightarrow{PR}=\begin{vmatrix}\mathbf{i}&\mathbf{j}&\mathbf{k}\\-1&1&-2\\-5&6&-8\end{vmatrix}$ or equivalent	
		$\bullet^5$	calculate normal	$\bullet^5$	$\mathbf{n}=\begin{pmatrix}4\\2\\-1\end{pmatrix}$	
		$\bullet^6$	obtain equation	$\bullet^6$	$4x+2y-z=1$	

Notes:
1.   Do not award $\bullet^4$ where the position vectors of P, Q or R are used.

Question			Generic scheme		Illustrative scheme	Max mark
(c)		$\bullet^7$	substitute into equation of plane	$\bullet^7$	$4(2\lambda+7)+2(6\lambda+8)-(-\lambda+1)=1$	3
		$\bullet^8$	find λ	$\bullet^8$	$\lambda=-2$	
		$\bullet^9$	determine coordinates of H [1]	$\bullet^9$	$\mathrm{H}(3,-4,3)$	

Notes:
1.   Do not accept a position vector at $\bullet^9$.

Question			Generic scheme		Illustrative scheme	Max mark
16.		$\bullet^1$	state form of integral [1,2,3]	$\bullet^1$	$V=\pi\int x^2\,dy$ or $V=\pi\int\left(f(y)\right)^2 dy$	5
		$\bullet^2$	rearrange and substitute for x^2	$\bullet^2$	$V=\pi\int\left(9-\frac{9}{4}y^2\right)dy$	
		$\bullet^3$	calculate limits to match variable [4]	$\bullet^3$	$\int_0^2\ldots dy$ or $y=0, y=2$	
		$\bullet^4$	integrate	$\bullet^4$	$V=\pi\left[9y-\frac{3y^3}{4}\right]_0^2$	
		$\bullet^5$	evaluate [5,6]	$\bullet^5$	$V=12\pi$ (cubic units)	

Notes:
1. dy must appear for $\bullet^1$ to be awarded.
2. $\bullet^1$ may be awarded at $\bullet^2$.
3.   For candidates who write $V=\pi\int x^2\,dx$, $V=\pi\int y^2\,dy$ or $V=\pi\int y^2\,dx$ and proceed to:

   (a) $V=\pi\int\left(9-\frac{9}{4}y^2\right)dy$ full credit may still be available

   (b) $V=\pi\int\left(4-\frac{4}{9}x^2\right)dx$ $\bullet^2$, $\bullet^3$, $\bullet^4$ and $\bullet^5$ may still be available

   (c) $\pi\left[\frac{x^3}{3}\right]$ or $\pi\left[\frac{y^3}{3}\right]$ only $\bullet^3$ is available

4. $\bullet^3$ may be awarded at $\bullet^4$.
5. $\bullet^5$ is not available where a candidate's evaluation necessarily leads to a negative answer.
6.   At $\bullet^5$ units are not required.

Question			Generic scheme		Illustrative scheme		Max mark
17.	(a)		$\bullet^1$	state second root	$\bullet^1$	$2-i$	1
	(b)		$\bullet^2$	obtain two linear actors	$\bullet^2$	$z-(2+i),\, z-(2-i)$	6
			$\bullet^3$	obtain quadratic factor	$\bullet^3$	z^2-4z+5	
			$\bullet^4$	set up algebraic division or equivalent	$\bullet^4$	$(z^2-4z+5)\,\overline{\left)\,z^4-6z^3+16z^2-22z+q\right.}$	
			$\bullet^5$	complete algebraic division	$\bullet^5$	$\begin{array}{r} z^2-2z+3 \\ z^2-4z+5\,\overline{\left)\,z^4-6z^3+16z^2-22z+q\right.} \\ z^4-4z^3+5z^2 \\ -2z^3+11z^2-22z+q \\ -2z^3+8z^2-10z \\ 3z^2-12z+q \\ 3z^2-12z+15 \\ q-15 \end{array}$	
			$\bullet^6$	state value of q [1,2]	$\bullet^6$	$q=15$	
			$\bullet^7$	obtain remaining two roots	$\bullet^7$	$1\pm\sqrt{2}\,i$	

Notes:
1. For candidates who substitute either $2+i$ or $2-i$ into the equation, obtain a correct value of q but who do not exhibit any other working, only $\bullet^6$ may be awarded.
2. $\bullet^6$ not available for a non-integer value of q.

Question			Generic scheme		Illustrative scheme		Max mark
17.	(c)		$\bullet^8$	show all four solutions on an Argand diagram [1,2,3,4]	$\bullet^8$		1

Question	Generic scheme	Illustrative scheme	Max mark

Notes:
1. Do not penalise the omission of the labels on the axes.
2. $\bullet^8$ is available only where 4 roots are illustrated.
3. Positional information is required for $\bullet^8$. In the illustrative scheme this is provided by the relative positions of the points. Where points are plotted inaccurately, positional information may be provided by coordinates e.g. $(2,1)$ or the numbers 2 and 1 indicated on the appropriate axes. Accept $(2,i)$. The label $2+i$ is not of itself sufficient to award $\bullet^8$.

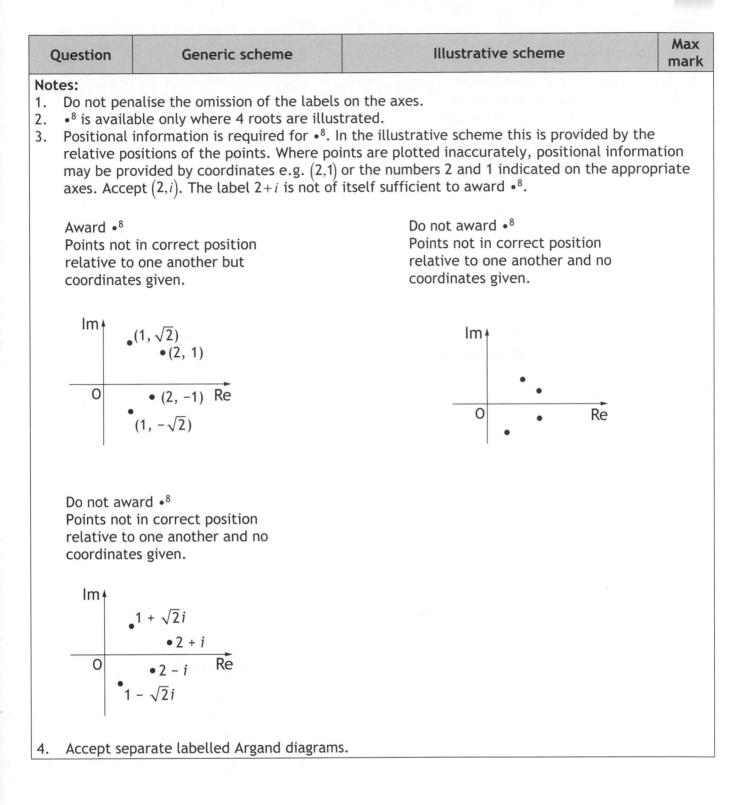

Award $\bullet^8$
Points not in correct position relative to one another but coordinates given.

Do not award $\bullet^8$
Points not in correct position relative to one another and no coordinates given.

Do not award $\bullet^8$
Points not in correct position relative to one another and no coordinates given.

4. Accept separate labelled Argand diagrams.

Question	Generic scheme	Illustrative scheme	Max mark
18. (a)	[1] evidence of use of product rule to find either $\frac{dx}{dt}$ or $\frac{dy}{dt}$ with one term correct	[1] e.g. $\frac{dx}{dt} = \cos t + \ldots$	5
	[2] obtain $\frac{dx}{dt}$ or $\frac{dy}{dt}$	[2] $\frac{dx}{dt} = \cos t - t\sin t$	
	[3] obtain remaining derivative	[3] $\frac{dy}{dt} = \sin t + t\cos t$	
	[4] state formula for instantaneous speed	[4] speed $= \sqrt{\left(\frac{dx}{dt}\right)^2 + \left(\frac{dy}{dt}\right)^2}$ stated or implied at [5]	
	[5] obtain expression [1,2]	[5] $\sqrt{\left(\cos t - t\sin t\right)^2 + \left(\sin t + t\cos t\right)^2}$ $= \sqrt{1+t^2}$	

Notes:
1. At [5] the simplification to $\sqrt{1+t^2}$ is not required.
2. [5] may only be awarded for substitution into an expression of the form $\sqrt{\left(\ldots\right)^2 + \left(\ldots\right)^2}$.

Question	Generic scheme	Illustrative scheme	Max mark
(b)	[6] evidence of valid strategy to find value of t and obtain at least one non-zero solution [1]	[6] $0 = t\sin t$ and e.g. $t = \pi$	2
	[7] choose correct value for t and calculate speed [1,2]	[7] $t = 3\pi$ speed $= \sqrt{1+9\pi^2}$	

Notes:
1. For candidates who obtain an expression for $\frac{dy}{dx}$ rather than instantaneous speed, [6] and [7] are still available.
2. At [7] accept a decimal answer provided it is accurate to at least 3sf (9·48).

Acknowledgements

Hodder Gibson would like to thank the SQA for use of any past exam questions that may have been used in model papers, whether amended or in original form.